Chords for
Rock and Blues Guitar

By Ed Lozano with Jon Griffin

© 2019 HJJ Publishing
http://hjjpublishing.com/
Las Vegas NV
Made in USA
All Rights Reserved

ISBN-13: 978-1941837559
ISBN-10: 1-941837-55-7

Contents

Rock and Blues Chords for Guitar

Introduction

Many beginning players struggle with the one element that all songs are made up of—chords. There are two main points that confuse aspiring players. First, there are those big chord encyclopedias with dozens of permutations for one simple chord symbol. Second, many songbooks will always contain a new chord symbol that these new players simply don't understand. Both which lead to guitar parts that sound nothing like the original recording.

Guitarists can learn in two different ways: Study or trial and error. The only trouble is, sometimes the chords you study aren't the same as the ones you actually use when you're playing. The purpose of this chart is to guide you through the chord shapes which guitarists use most of the time. It's not intended to cover every chord that was ever invented—there's no chapter on jazz, for example—but it does contain the shapes that the majority of working guitarists use when they're playing live or recording.

Diagrams Explained

Chords are written in diagram form or standard music notation and tablature. Let's take a closer look at these methods of notation.

Fretboxes

Fretboxes show the guitar upright i.e. with the headstock, nut and tuning pegs at the top of the picture-six vertical lines represent the strings.

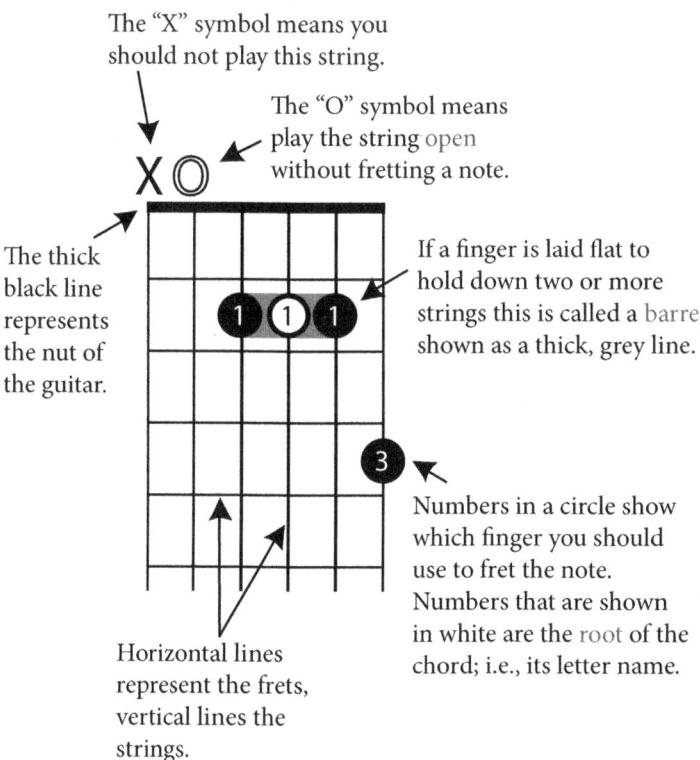

The "X" symbol means you should not play this string.

The "O" symbol means play the string open without fretting a note.

The thick black line represents the nut of the guitar.

If a finger is laid flat to hold down two or more strings this is called a barre, shown as a thick, grey line.

Numbers in a circle show which finger you should use to fret the note. Numbers that are shown in white are the root of the chord; i.e., its letter name.

Horizontal lines represent the frets, vertical lines the strings.

Standard Notation and Tablature

Tab is drawn with the guitar on its side, with the thickest string at the bottom—six horizontal lines represent the strings.

The top staff shows the chord as it would appear in traditional music notation.

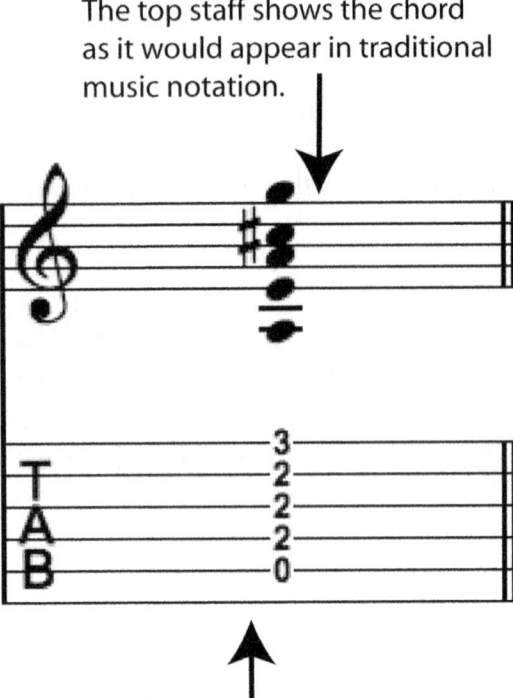

This is the tablature; the numbers represent the fret positions. A "0" means the string should be played open.

Open Major Chords

One of the simplest and most common types of chord is the major. They have a very simple, uncomplicated sound, and as such are often used in folk and country music. The major chords in this section are played in an *open* position, meaning that one or more of the strings you strum is not fretted. Open chords are, most of the time, the easiest type to play.

You can hear major chords in almost every type of music. These examples have all been used at one time or another by artists as diverse as Buddy Holly, the Beatles, Bob Dylan, The Eagles, Queen and Led Zeppelin. In gig set lists and chord charts, they're generally referred to by their letter name only, so the word major is omitted; *e.g.*, C major is usually referred to just as C.

A

Don't strum the sixth (thickest) string. You may find it tricky to squeeze three fingers together in a row like this—many rock players cover all three notes by squeezing the second and third fingers together.

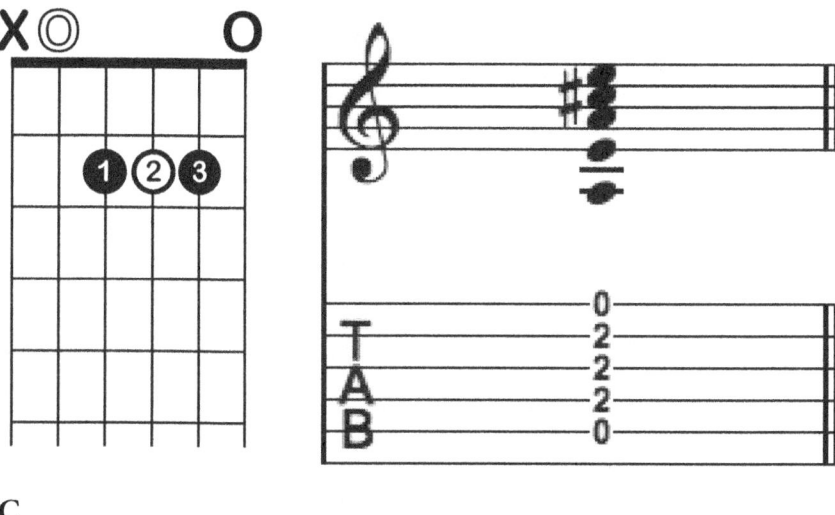

C

C is more difficult because one of the open strings occurs between the fretted notes. Keep all your fingers at right angles to the fingerboard to let the open strings ring freely.

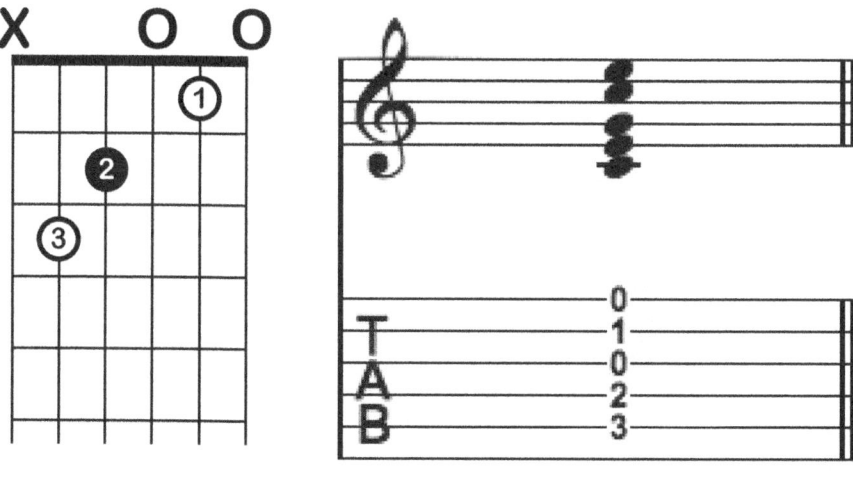

Quick Tip

A voicing is the simultaneous vertical placement of notes in relation to each other or the order of notes from top to bottom. Sometimes called an inversion, the difference being that inversion refers specifically to the note in the bass (or at the bottom of the chord). Whereas the term voicing refers to the melody as is presented in the following example.

C (alternate version)

This version of the open C chord has a slightly fuller sound due to the top G note which is added by the little finger. It's often used by folk-rock acoustic players like Bob Dylan and Paul Simon.

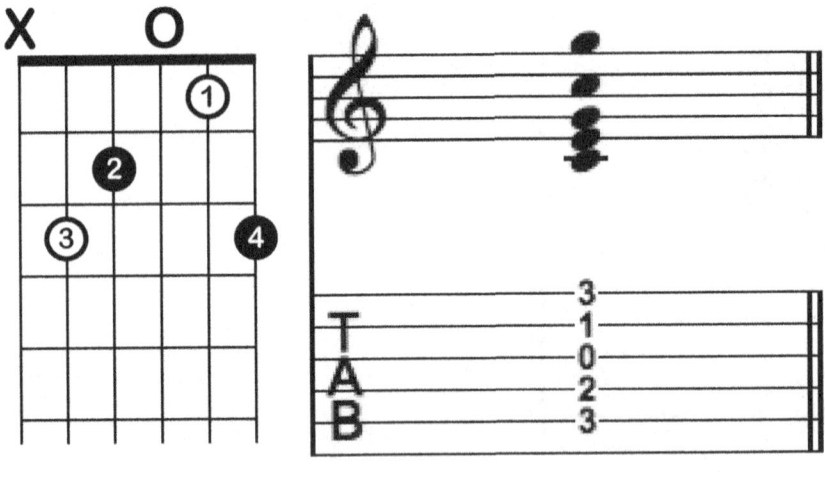

D

Most players think of D as a triangle shape on the neck. Avoid strumming the sixth and fifth strings.

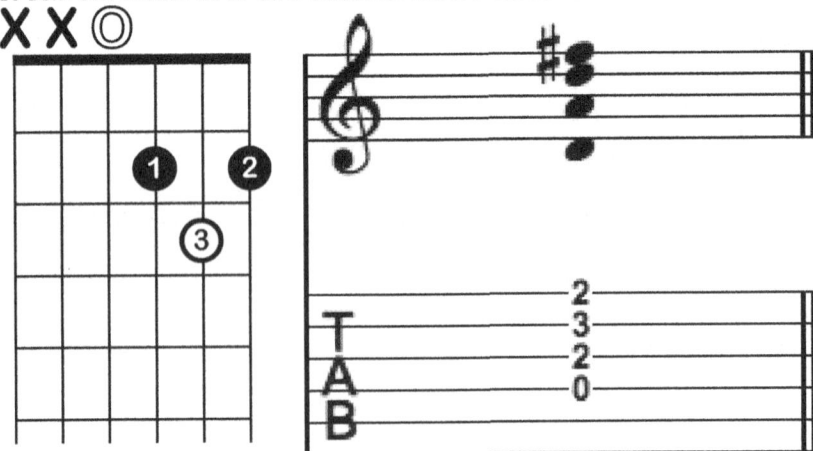

E

E has a rich, full sound, because it contains three open notes, and you can strum all six strings.

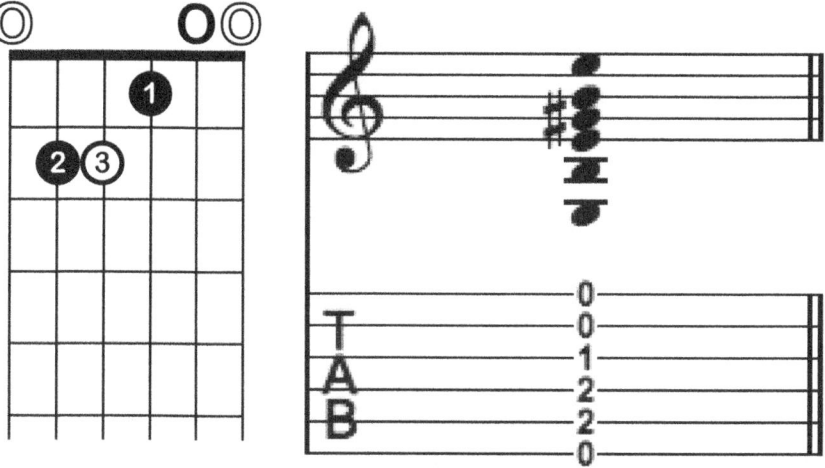

F

Although not strictly an open chord (*i.e.* it doesn't contain open strings) this easy F is shown here because of its 1st fret position. Note that the first finger is flattened across two strings in a barre.

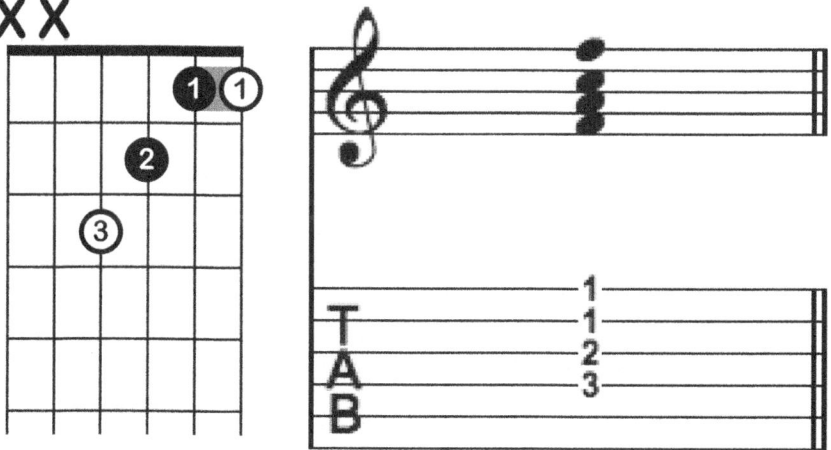

G is another full-sounding chord, but it can take work to master the stretch between the second and third fingers. Make sure that you don't accidentally mute any of the open strings.

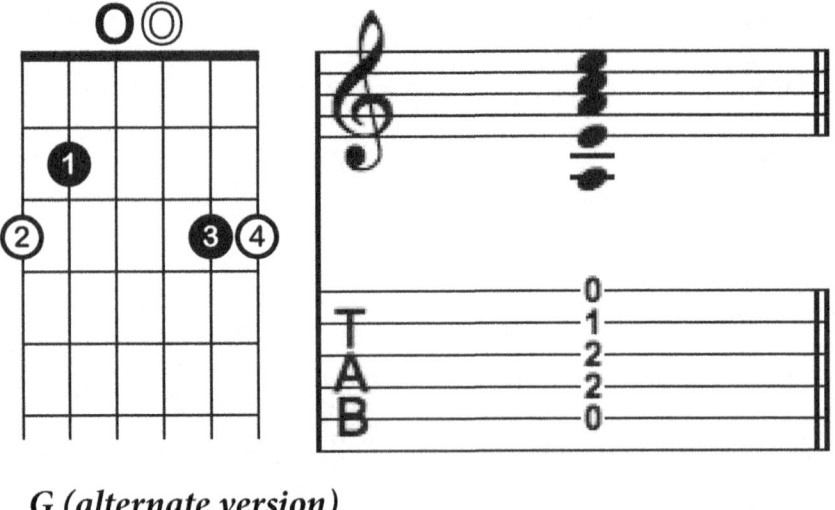

G (alternate version)

Some guitarists play a G chord with four fingers, as shown here. It gives more of a rock feel, and you'll see it under the fingers of Tom Petty and Bruce Springsteen, among others.

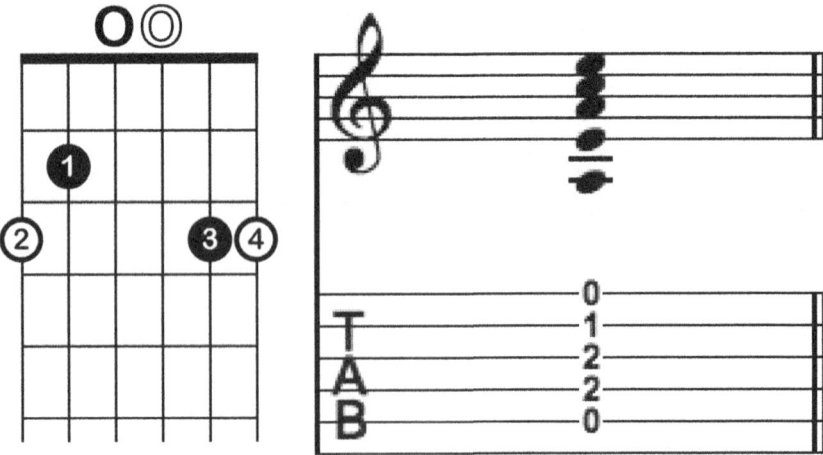

Open Minor Chords

If every songwriter only ever played major chords, the world would never have heard Led Zeppelin's "Stairway to Heaven," John Lennon's "Working Class Hero" or Metallica's "Nothing Else Matters." Minor chords have a melancholy edge which some musicians describe as sad sounding, although this isn't always the case—check out the up-tempo verse of "I Wanna Be Like You" from the movie *The Jungle Book*, or the intro from the blues classic "Hit The Road Jack."

The three minor chords shown here have been used in thousands of songs, and are among the first chords every guitar player needs to learn. Usually, they are combined with other types of chords (such as majors, dominant 7s, minor 7s, *etc.*)—it's rare for a piece of music to feature minor chords only. In some of the songs reference below you'll find all three of the main chord qualities represented (major, minor, and dominant).

Am

This is the first chord in The Animals' "House of the Rising Sun" and The Rolling Stones' "Angie," among many others. Make sure you don't play the sixth string accidentally—this will make the chord sound muddy.

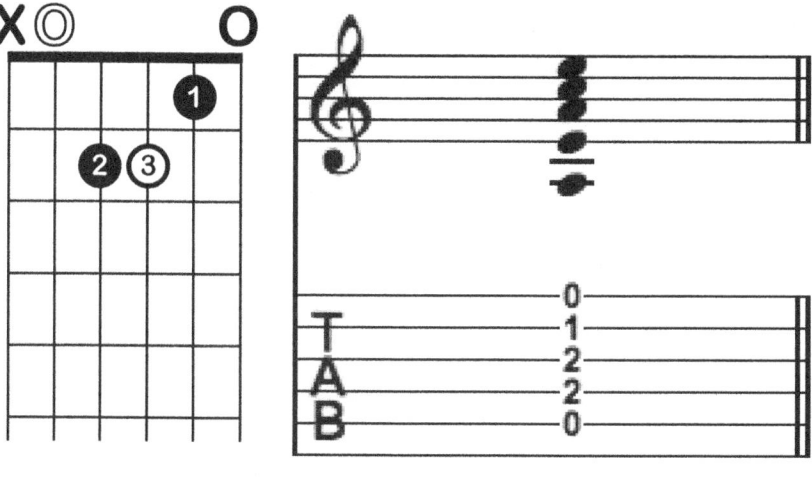

Dm

Although D minor is only a four-string chord (don't strum the two bass strings) it has a slightly sweeter sound than A minor. Practice it until all four strings sound clearly.

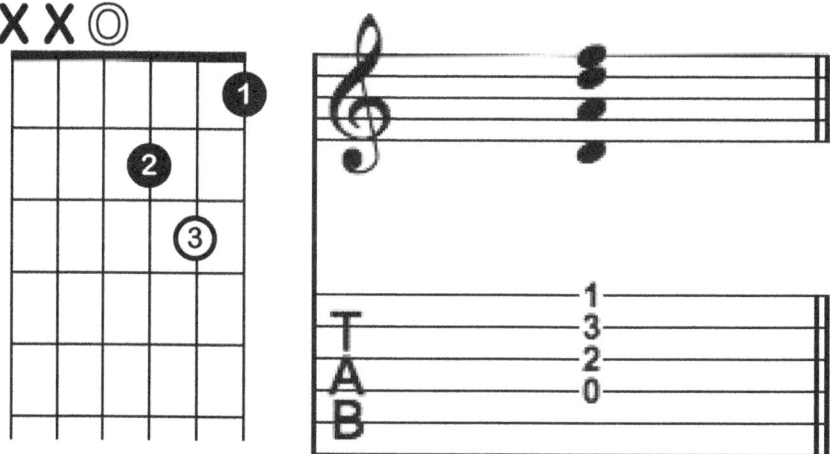

Em

This dramatic-sounding chord is the easiest of the three minor shapes. As long as you make sure that both fingers are cleanly and accurately fretting the notes, E minor will always sound great.

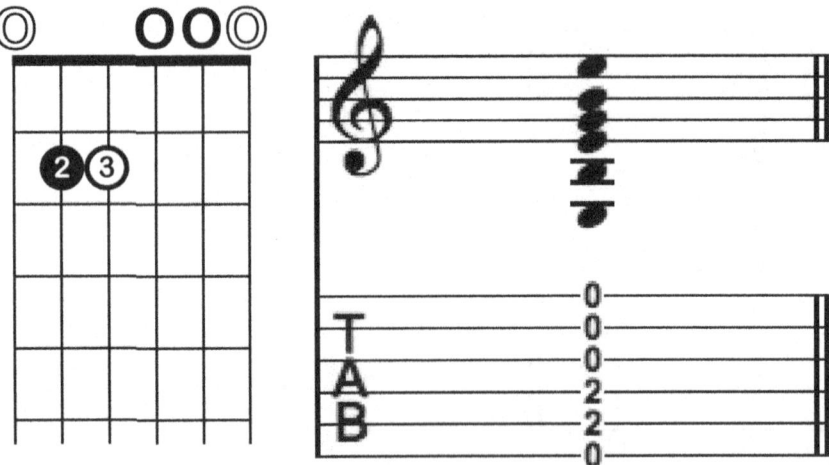

Open Seventh Chords

Seventh chords sound more complicated and colorful than their major and minor cousins. They come in three basic types: 7s (sometimes called dominant 7s), major 7s, and minor 7s. You may notice that some of the major 7-style shapes are similar to their corresponding major chord, and some of the minor 7s are similar to their corresponding minor chord. For this reason, 7-type chords are often used in place of more straightforward majors and minors.

Ordinary 7s sometimes appear in the blues, rock and R&B. Major 7s have a wistful quality and consequently sound good in ballads. Minor 7s can add a jazzy or funky sound to your chord sequence. Note the way they are abbreviated: 7, maj7 and m7. Again, the three basic chord qualities are represented here in 7-type chord form. If the 7 appears by itself it is understood that the quality of that chord is dominant.

A7

This is basically an ordinary A chord with one finger taken off, though feel free to use different fingers from the ones shown here if you find it easier to make the notes sound clearly.

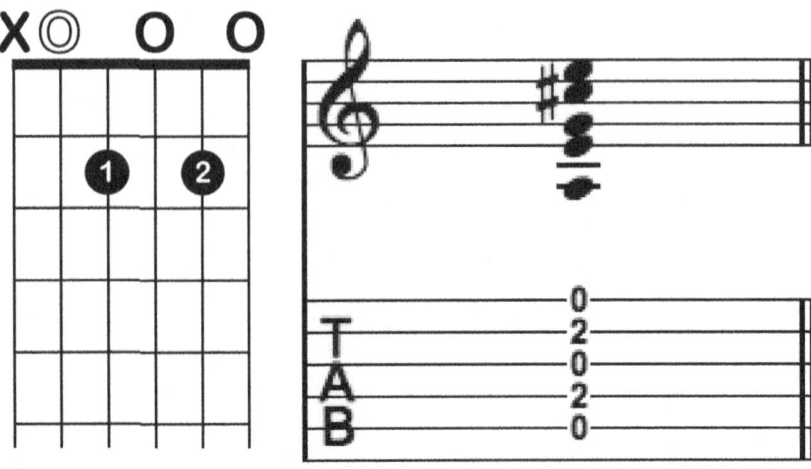

A7 (alternate version)

Although it's less common than the basic shape, many players still prefer this version of A7. It's tricky though, because you have to *barre* across three strings with the first finger.

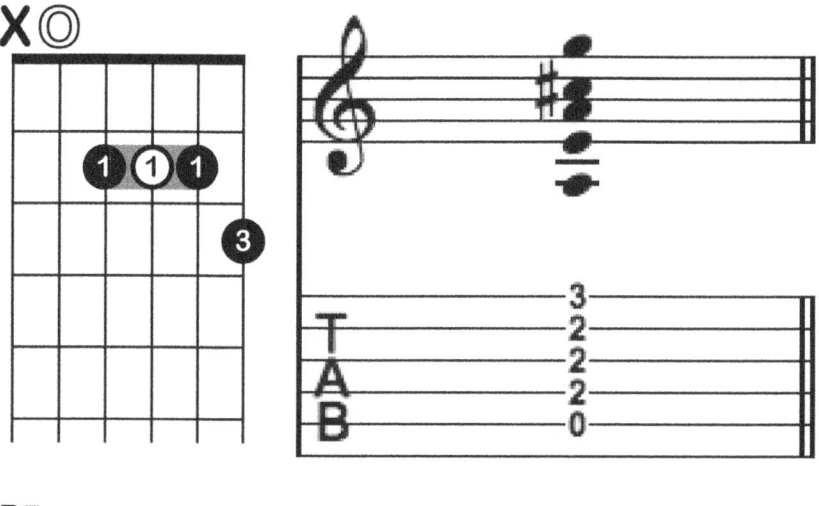

B7

Although it's not the easiest chord to play—the B7 is essential to learn—because it appears in the most common guitar-based chord sequence in the world: 12-bar blues in E.

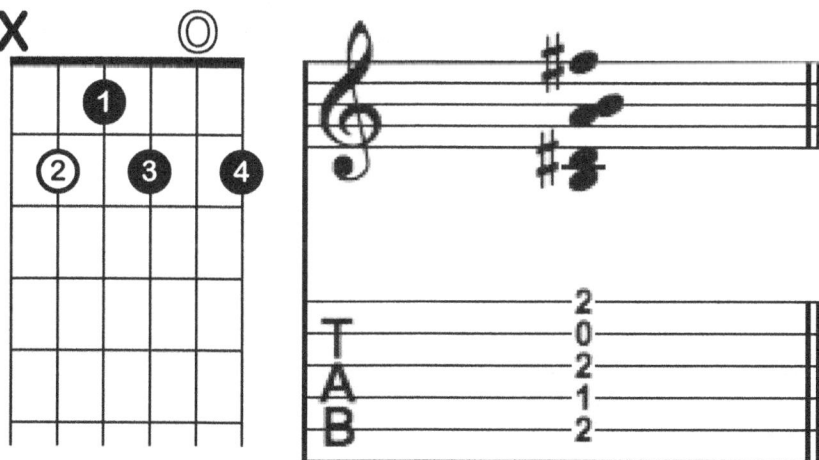

If you add your little finger to a normal C major chord you get this open version of C7. *Quick Tip:* Move this shape up two frets and play only the middle four strings for a different D7.

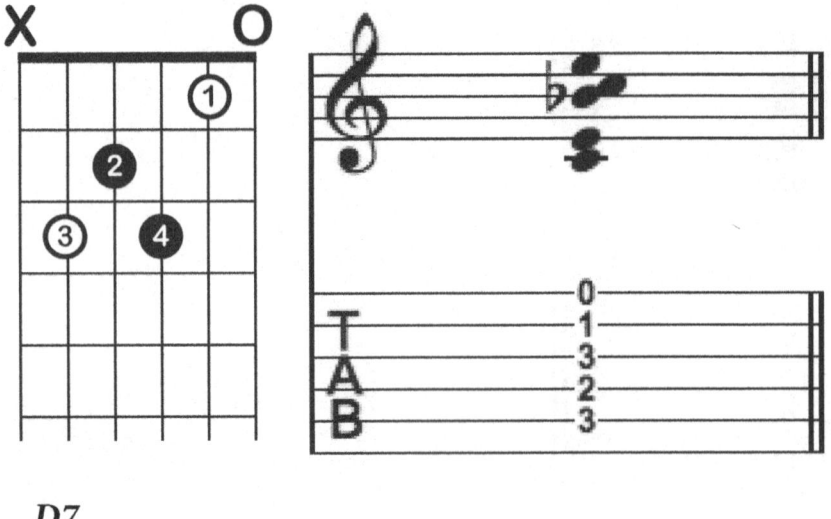

D7

This is the more common version of D7 though, as used by folk and delta blues players. It sounds very "country" if you play it before or after a G chord, or more bluesy when it occurs after an A7 chord.

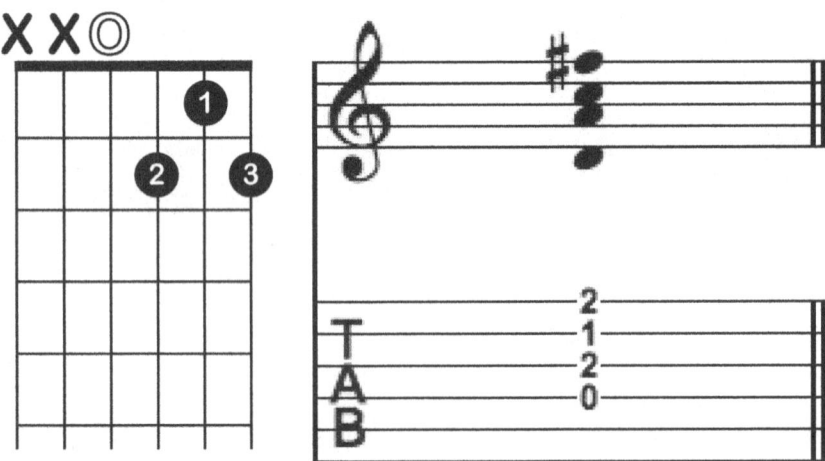

E7

If you're ever going to play the blues, you need this chord. It's another example of a major chord (E major) with a finger removed, creating a dominant 7. Make sure the open fourth string rings clearly.

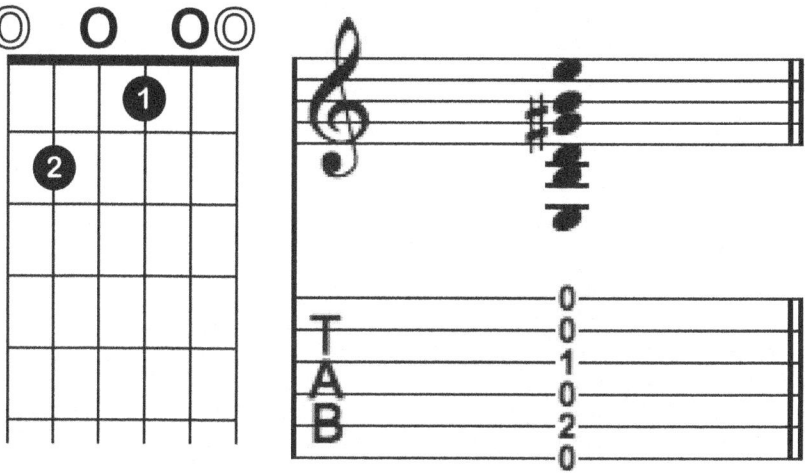

F♯7

Although you don't see this chord as often as some of the others in this section, it's a useful open chord in its own right—note that it's quite similar to the F shape in the "Open Major Chords" section.

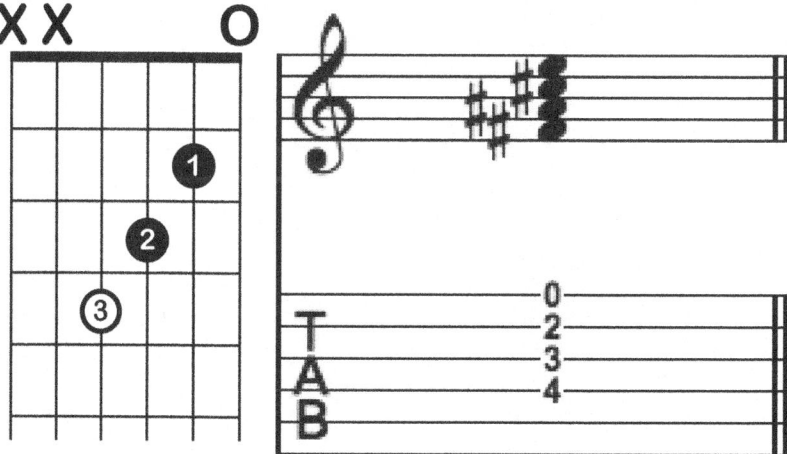

G7

The open chord of G7 looks similar to an ordinary G major ("Open Major Chords" section), but notice the variation to the fingering—you'll find that you have to move all three fingers to change between the chords of G and G7.

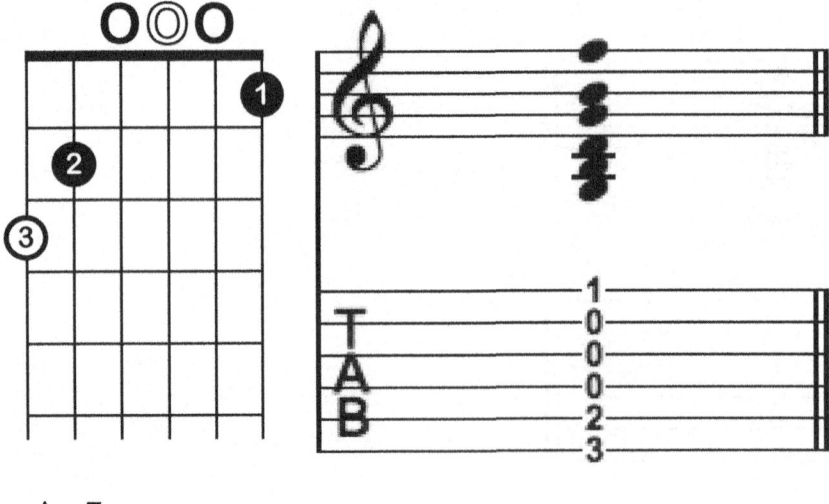

Am7

Take a finger off an A minor chord and you get an open Am7. Notice that the sixth string is not played.

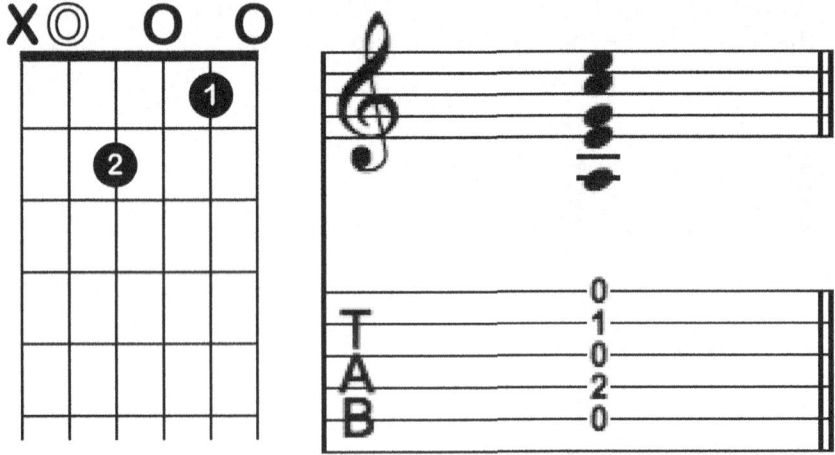

Dm7

This chord can be played with the first finger flattened over two strings, as shown here, or by using three separate fingers for the three fretted notes. This is the version most people find easiest.

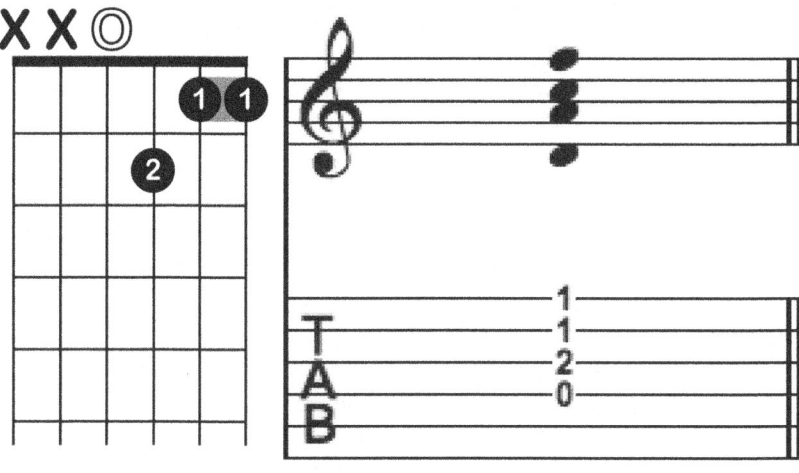

Em7

This very, simple chord is played using one finger and five open strings.

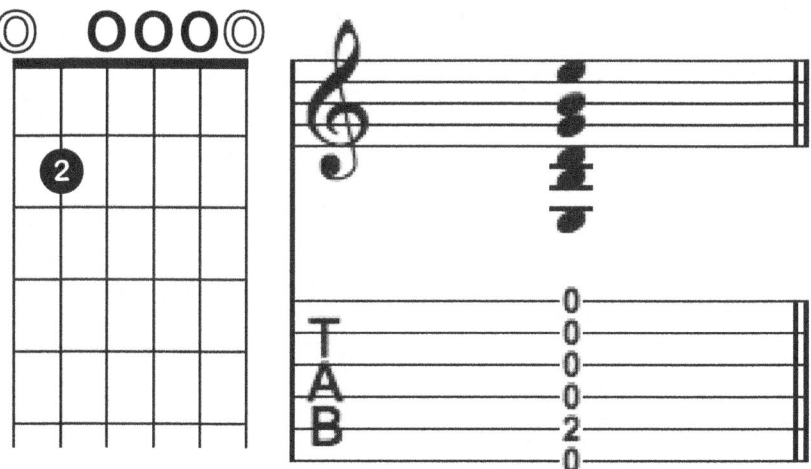

Amaj7

Although the fingering of this chord appears to be similar to the open D7 ("Open Seventh Chords" section), it sounds very different. Try playing a chord of A, followed by Amaj7, followed by A7 for a classic Beatles effect.

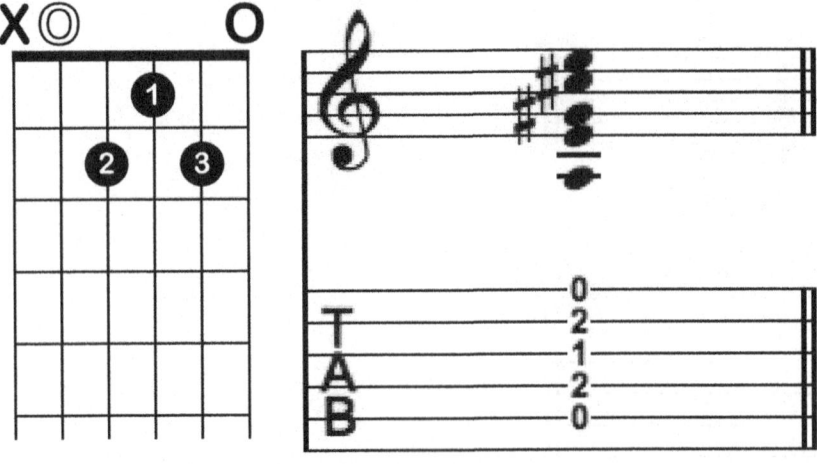

Cmaj7

Play a C chord, then remove the first finger, letting the open second string sound as shown.

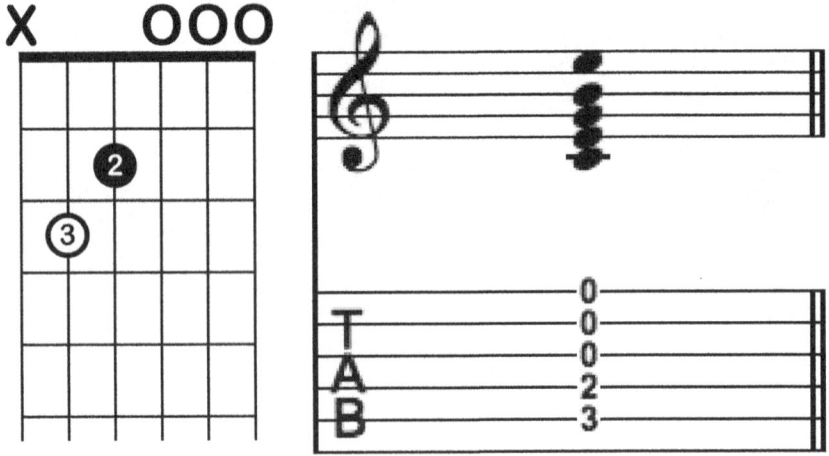

Dmaj7

Dmaj7 can be played either of two ways—with three separate fingers, as shown here, or with one finger flattened across the first three strings. Make sure the open fourth string rings clearly.

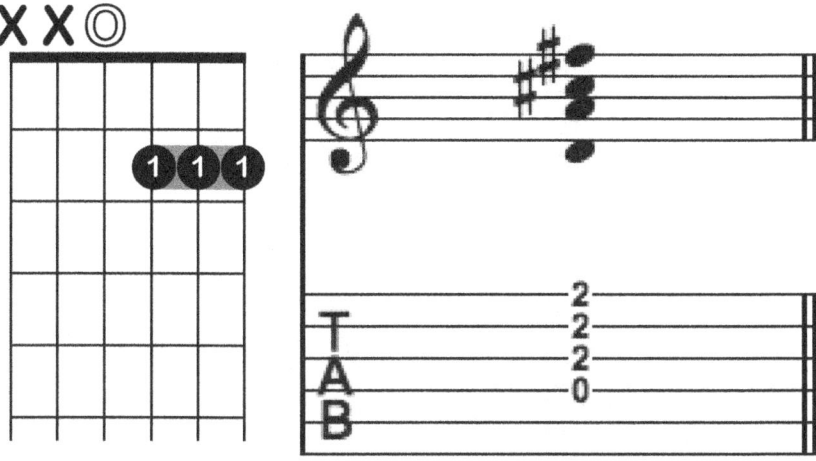

Emaj7

This open maj7 shape is not used by many players because it sometimes some unpleasant to the ear, but there are times (especially in country strumming or single-note, picked chord parts) when it works fine.

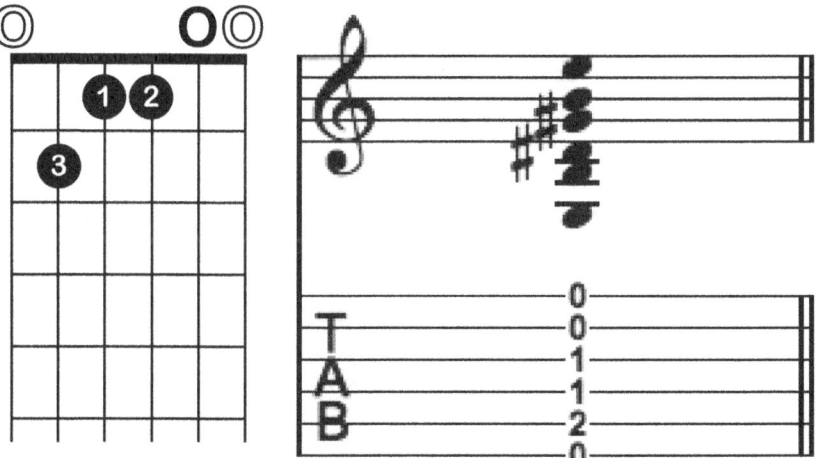

Fmaj7

This "diagonal" shape sounds lovely when it's played before or after a C or Cmaj7 chord.

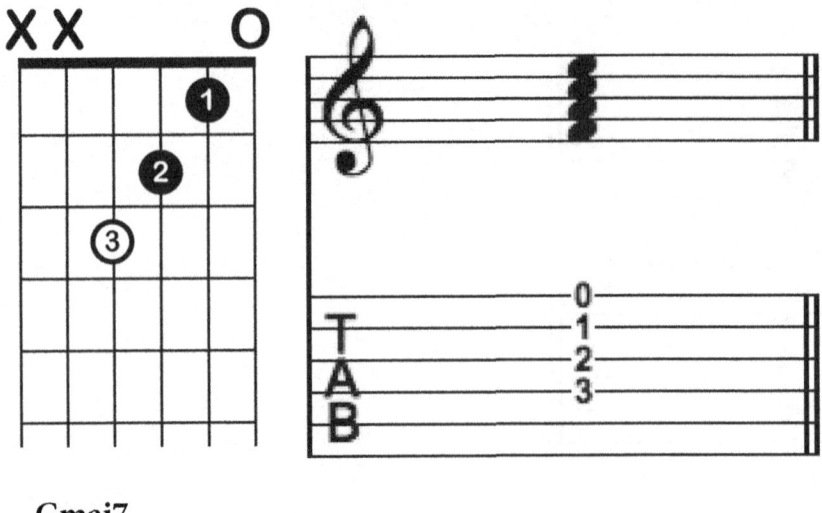

Gmaj7

This is the big, expansive chord that is played in the verse of The Eagles' track "Lyin' Eyes."

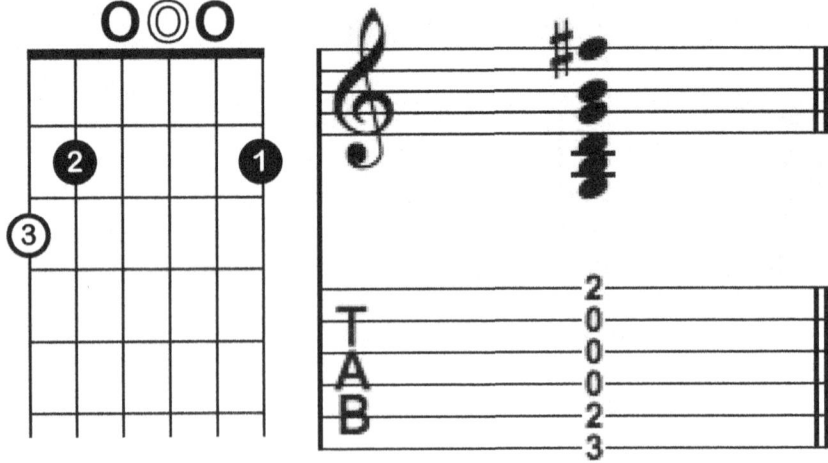

Barre Chords

Barre chords are so-called because one of the fretting hand's fingers is pressed against two or more strings (this is shown as a thick, grey line in the fretbox). They can be moved up or down the neck to create new chords. The advantage of this is that once you've learned one new barre shape, you've in effect learned 12 new chords.

Below are diagrams showing the names of the notes on the sixth and fifth strings. To find any barre chord, look at the fretbox to see whether the root note (shown in a white circle) appears on the fifth or sixth string, then move the barre shape up or down until you reach the desired pitch. For example, a chord of A♭ (also known as G♯) can be played using the *F shape* moved up to the 4th fret.

Sharps

This diagram shows how to find any barre-chord position, and will help you if the chord you want has a sharp (♯) in its name. All of the F-based barre shapes in this book (see below) have their root on the sixth string—the B♭-based ones have theirs on the fifth.

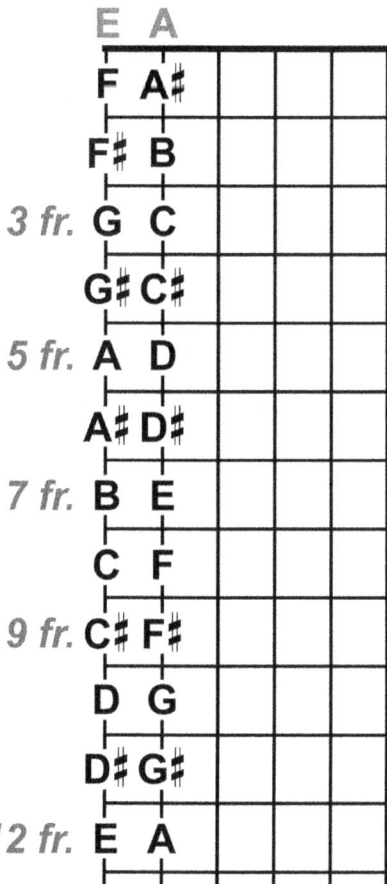

Flats

Use this version if the chord you want has a flat (♭) in its name. Both of these diagrams can be used to find any barre chord which has its roots on the sixth or fifth string-simply select the type you want (minor, maj7, 7 etc) then find the letter name (F,G,D etc) on the fingerboard.

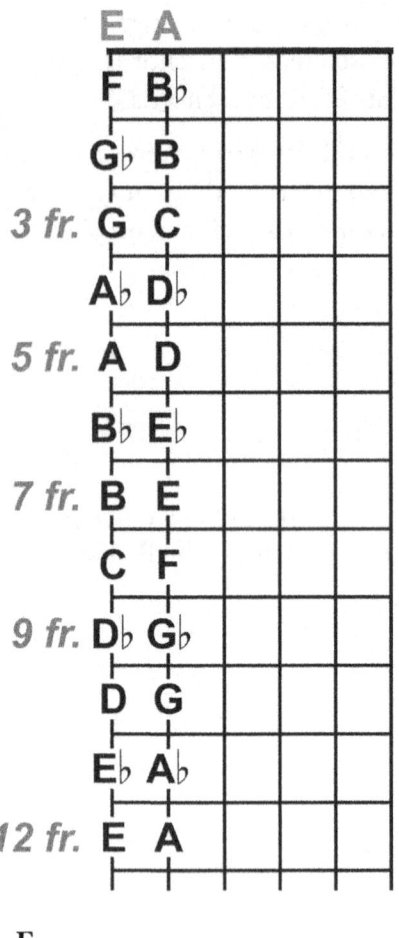

F

The F barre shape has its root on the sixth string. Move it up one fret to create an F♯, up two frets to create G. You can even play it way up at the 12th fret to create a barre chord of E.

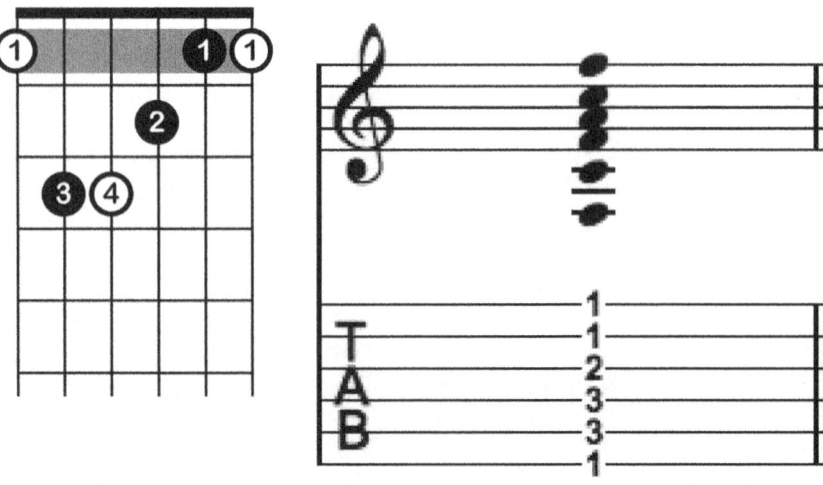

B♭

Any B♭-based barre shape has its root on the fifth string. Sometimes, if you're changing chords quickly, it's easier to change between the F and B♭ shapes because it involves less hand movement.

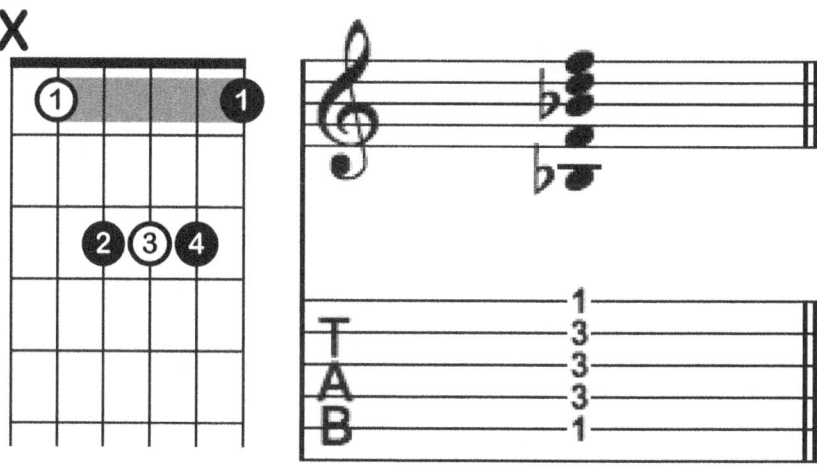

B♭ (alternate version)

Lots of rock and blues players favor this version of B♭—it sounds nearly as full, and is far easier to play. Make sure that you don't flatten the finger all the way over; the first string should not sound.

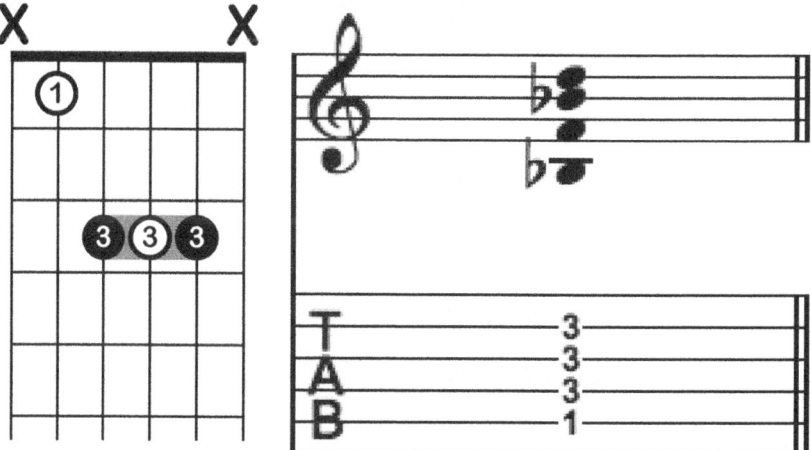

Fm

For this, the same principle applies as for the F major shape—move it up one fret to create F#m, move it up one more to create Gm, and so on all the way up to Em at the 12th fret.

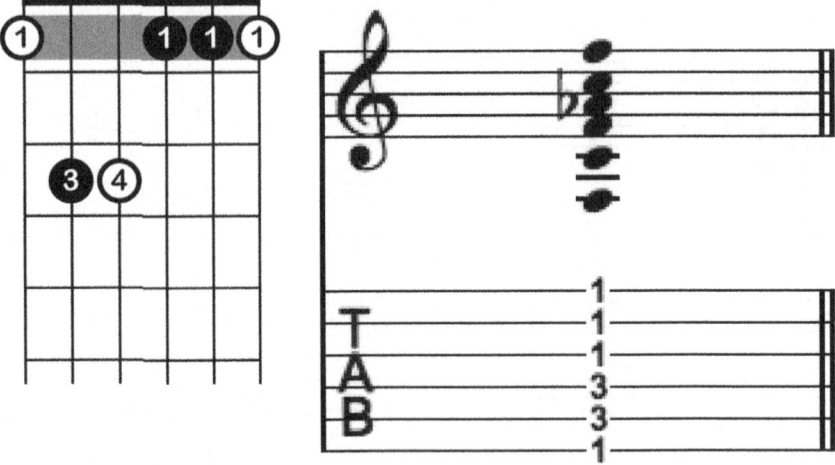

B♭m

This minor shape has its root on the 5th string, so to create a chord of Bm simply move up to the 2nd fret, Cm at the 3rd *etc*. Its sweet tone makes it especially good for funk, jazz and dance music.

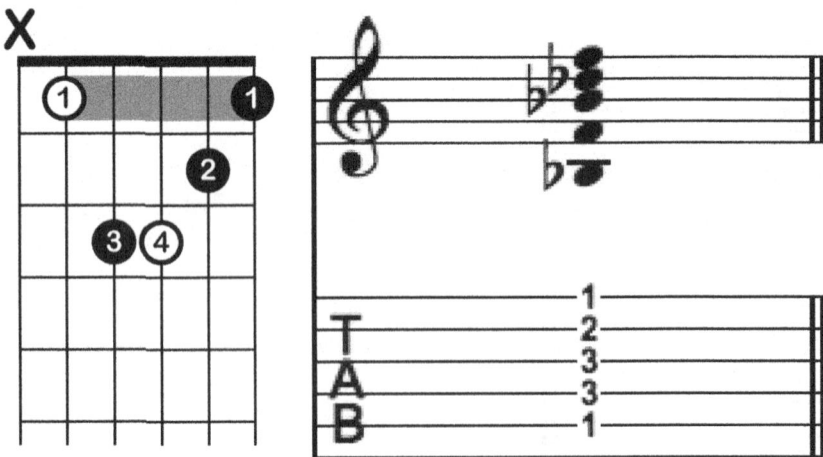

F7

Although this barre version of F7 looks very similar to the ordinary barre F shape, it's quite difficult to make that barred fourth string sound clearly in the middle of the chord.

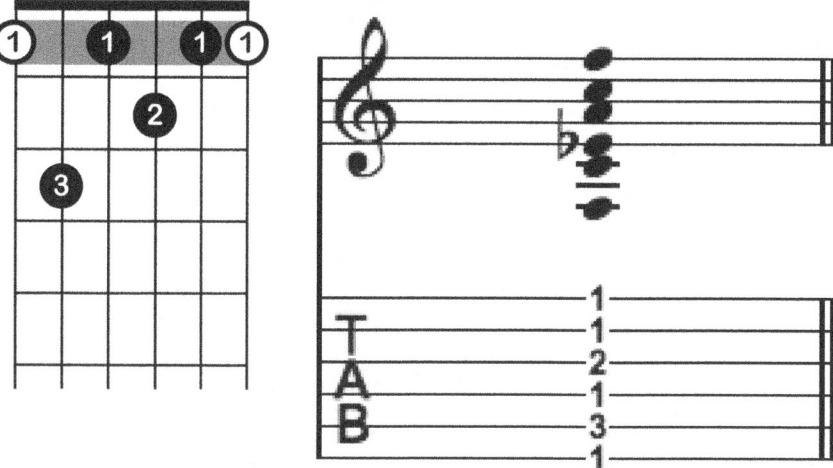

F7 (alternate version)

Add your little finger to the chord and you get this more colorful-sounding version of F7. It's a tricky stretch though, so ensure that all of the notes sound clearly as you strum across it.

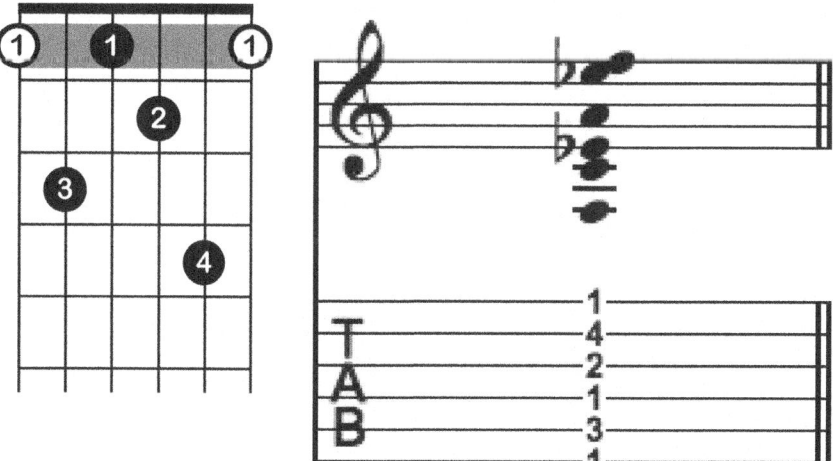

B♭7

This is a barre version of the ordinary open A7 shape. Note that the root is on the fifth string. This means that there's a chord of B7 at the 2nd fret, C7 at the 3rd, and A7 up at the 12th.

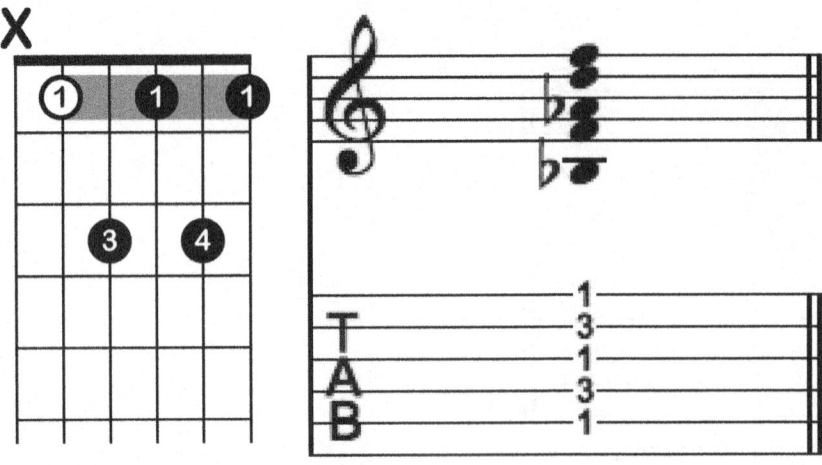

Fmaj7

Many players like to omit the first string when they play this chord because it clashes a bit with the note on the fourth string. Like all the other chords in this section, it can be moved to any fret.

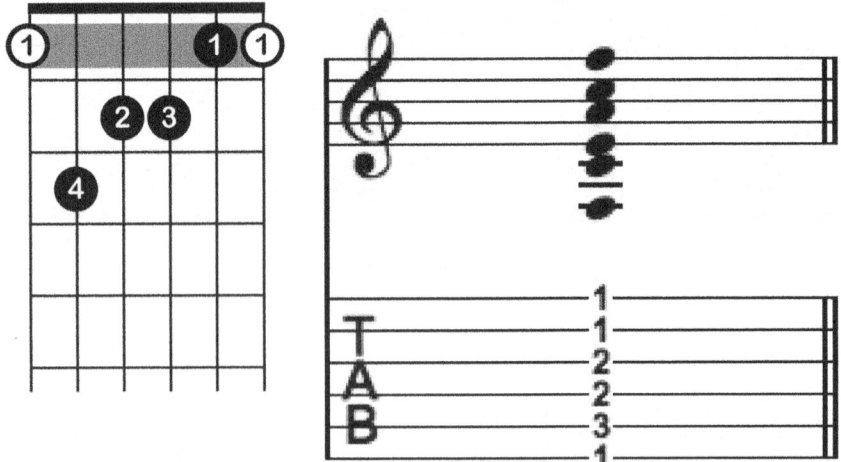

B♭maj7

This version of the major seventh barre chord is more common, and sounds "sweeter" than the F shape above. Note that the barre doesn't have to press all the strings—just the fifth and first.

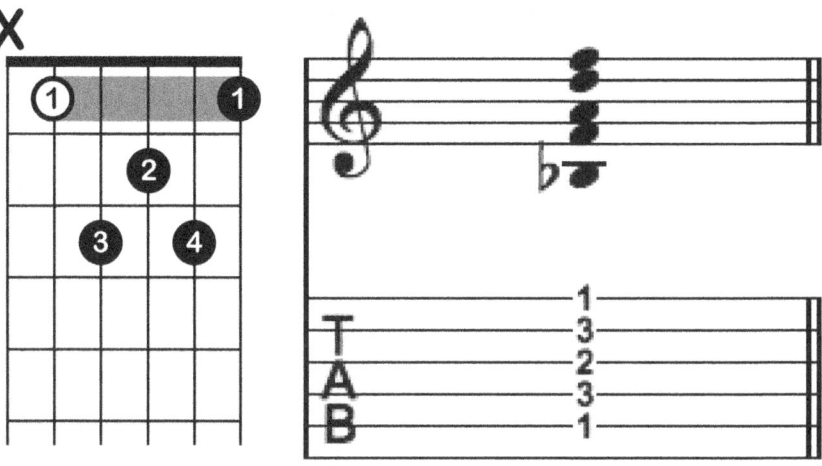

Fm7

Another six-string chord, this time with a barre covering all but one of the strings. Some funk players choose a "partial chord" version, just using the first finger flattened over the first three strings.

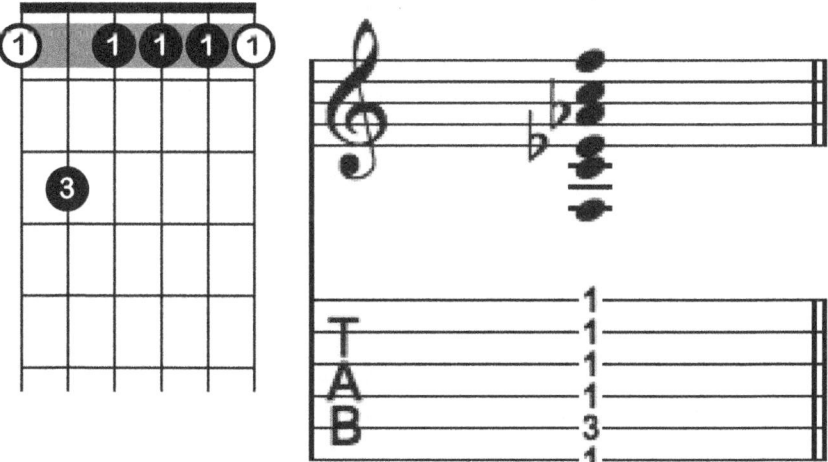

B♭m7

This difficult but versatile chord shape sounds just as good at the 13th fret as it does at the 1st. Try sliding into it as you strum rhythmic patterns for a funky 1970s disco sound.

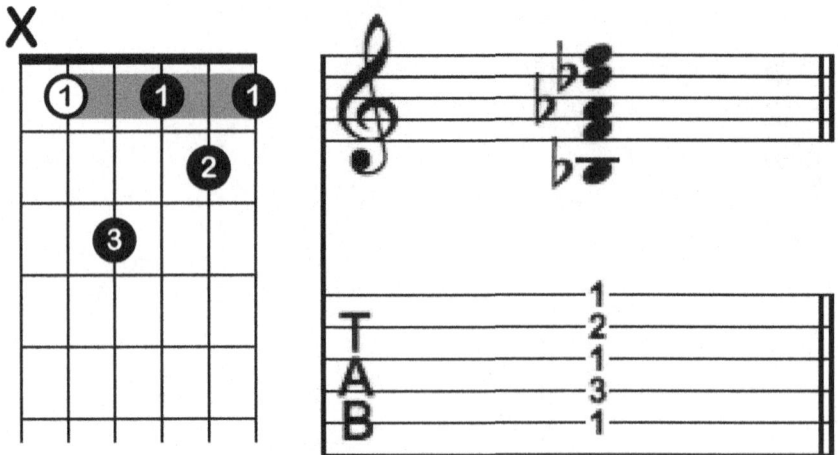

Power Chord

Power chords (also called 5 chords) are the sound behind almost every rock and metal band from Black Sabbath to Metallica. They have a strident, aggressive feel, and sound good with lots of distortion (try comparing an F5 power chord and an F major with the overdrive levels cranked right up—the F5 creates a more powerful sound). As with the barre chords in the previous section, the F and B♭ versions of the chords can be moved up to any fret using the fingerboard diagrams in the "Barre Chords" section; however, there are some great examples which feature open strings, and those chords have been included here too. Power chords are also useful for making up your own rock riffs—try moving the chord around the neck while you play downstrokes on the bass strings with the pick.

F5

With this movable power chord there are two choices: Either play the three bass strings as shown, or only hit the sixth and fifth strings. Remember to mute the other three strings.

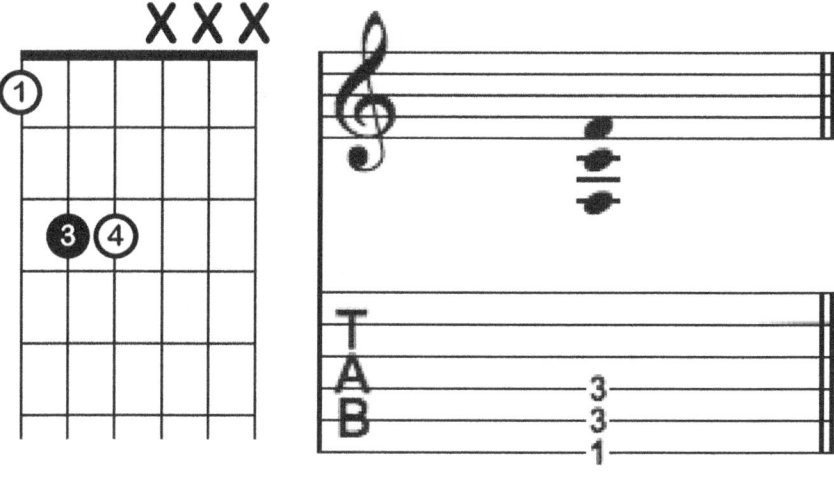

B♭5

Sometimes you may not need to move the F5 shape all over the neck—there may be a version of the power chord you want with its root on the fifth string.

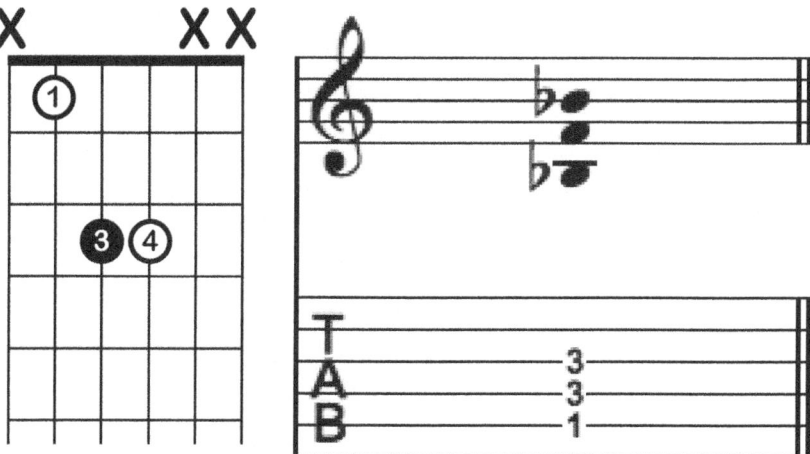

A5

This open power chord appears at the beginning of "Won't Get Fooled Again" by The Who, "Tie Your Mother Down" by Queen, plus many bar-blues standards. It's a stripped-down version of the A major.

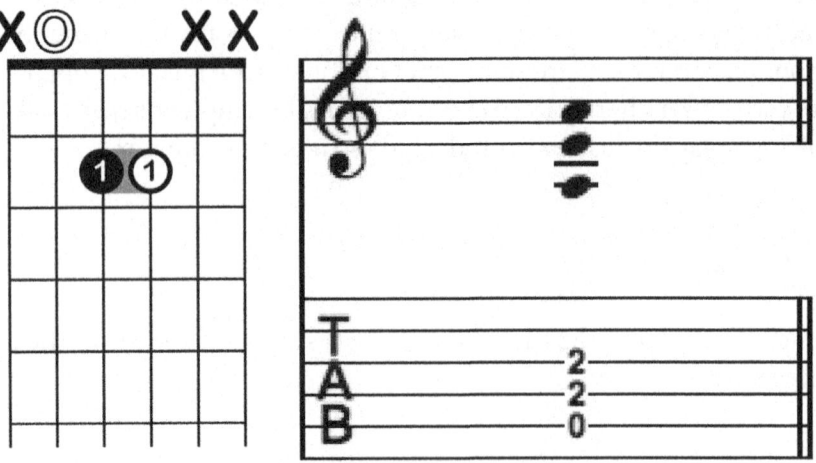

A5 (alternate version)

This version of A5 covers three octaves, so it has an even more powerful sound. You may have trouble flattening the little finger over two strings.

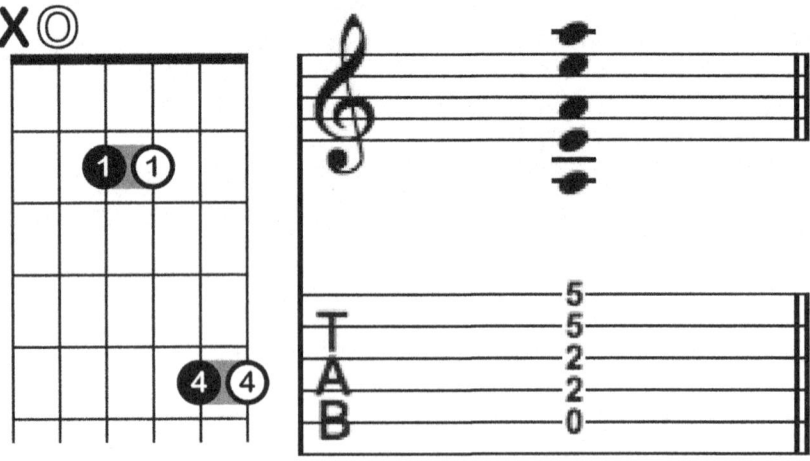

C5

Although this is not a commonly-used shape, it's interesting, because it uses muting techniques to stop some strings from sounding. Famously used in ZZ Top's "Gimme All your Lovin.'"

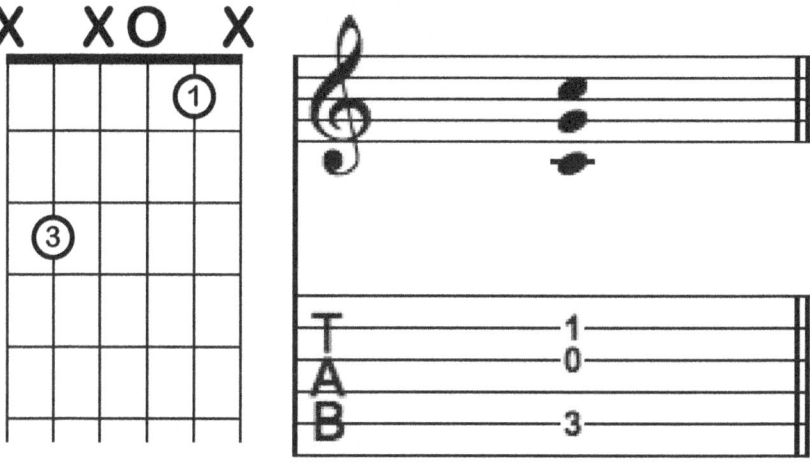

D5

Like the open A5 above, this is just a simplified version of the equivalent major chord. You might find though, that in a fretted version (B5 shape at the 5th fret) sounds more convincing.

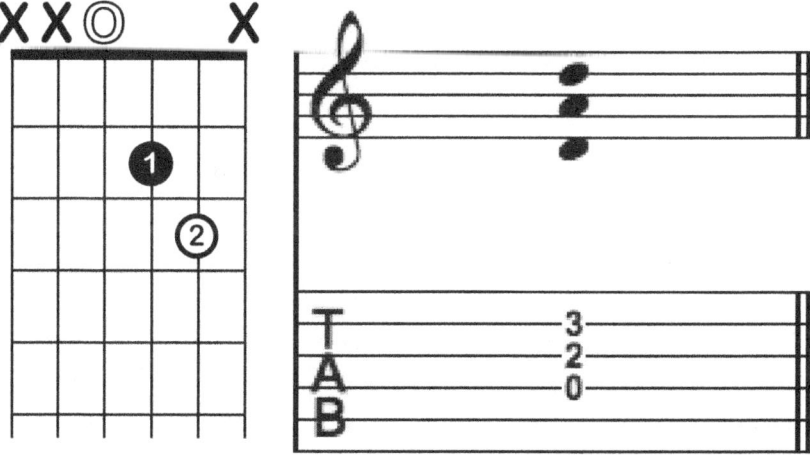

D5 (alternate version)

Here's a more spaced-out version of the same chord from the previous example. Try adding distortion and delay, then picking across the strings one-by-one for a typical rock-anthem-type guitar intro.

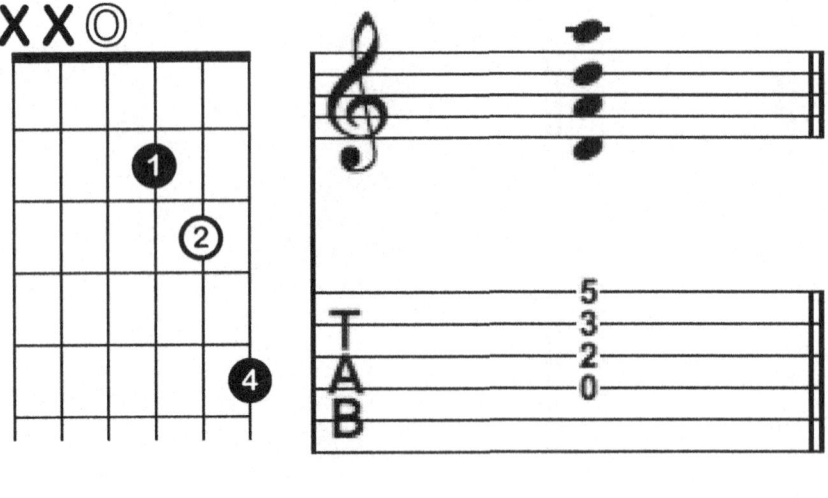

E5

This is the lowest, thickest-sounding power chord on the guitar fingerboard. It sounds great played with downstrokes as a rock or blues accompaniment part.

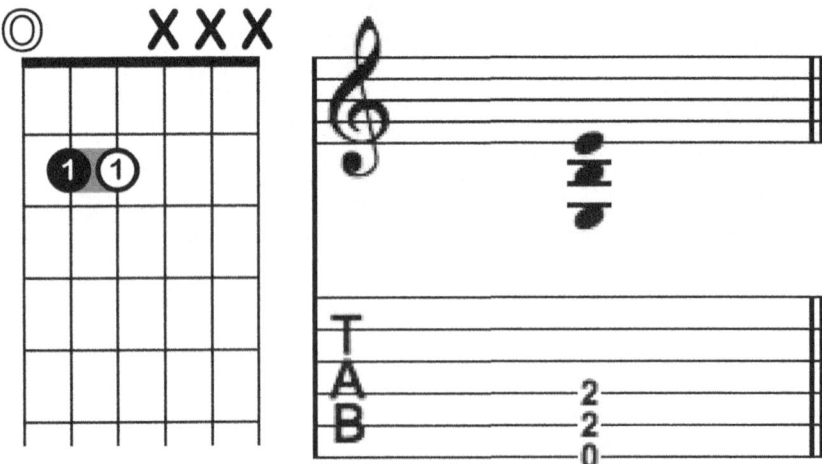

E5 (alternate version)

This is an expanded version of the more common three-string version (above). The first and second strings can, if so desired, be played open for a more "jangly" sound.

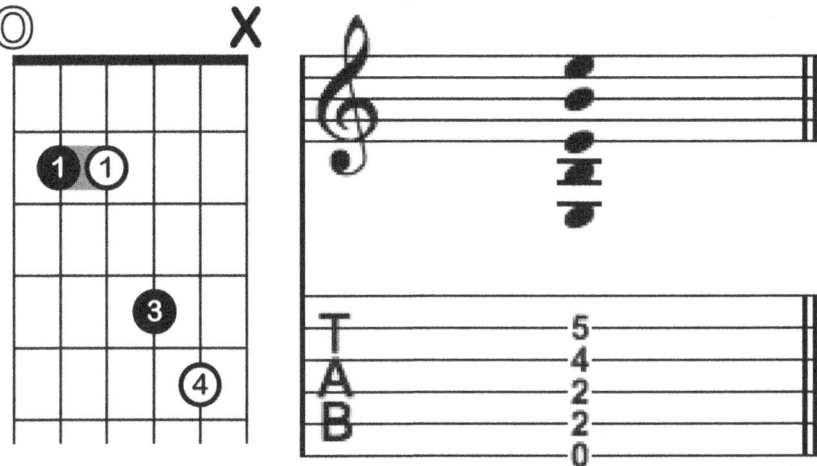

F5 (alternate version)

Although this version of F5 is movable, its root is actually on the fourth string. So it creates G5 when played at the 5th fret, A♭5 at the 6th, and D5 way up at the 12th.

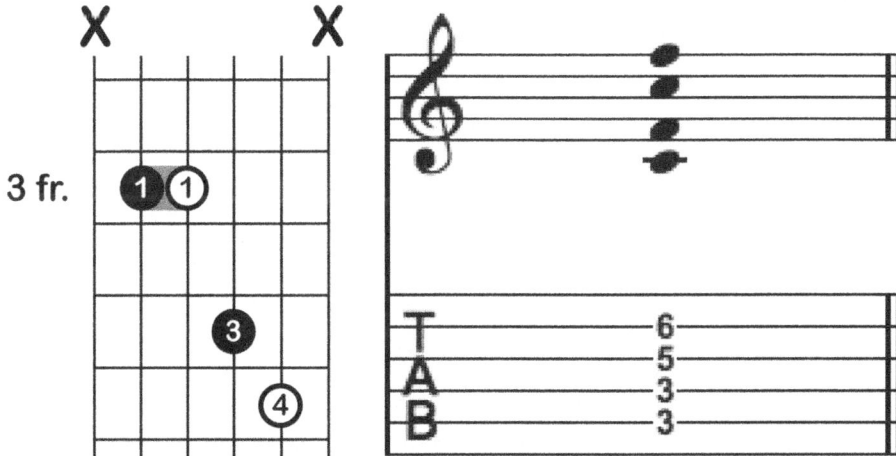

G5

If you omit the 5th string from the easy G major chord in the "Open Major Chords" section, you get this powerful alternative to a G5 barre shape. Use the side of the second finger to mute the 5th string.

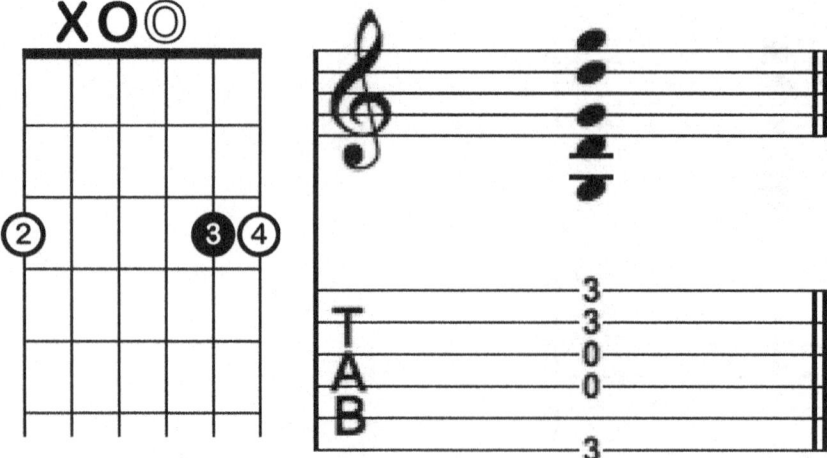

Suspended Chords

Suspended chords are so-called because one of the notes has been taken out and replaced with a different note which isn't a part of a major or minor chord—so a note is *suspended*. They create an unfinished, suspended-in-space effect. Sus chords, as they're known, come in two types: sus2 and sus4, of which sus4 is the most common. They are rarely used on their own and because of their incomplete sound they nearly always resolve to a more straightforward chord such as a major or minor. Check out the intro to The Who's "Pinball Wizard" (shown in the "Classic Chords" section) the strummed chords at the end of the chorus from The Beatles' "You've Got to Hide Your Love Away," or Led Zeppelin's "Stairway to Heaven."

Fsus4

This is the standard six-string sus4 with its root on the sixth string. As with all F-type barre chords, it can be moved to any fret position using the fingerboard diagrams from the "Barre Chords" section.

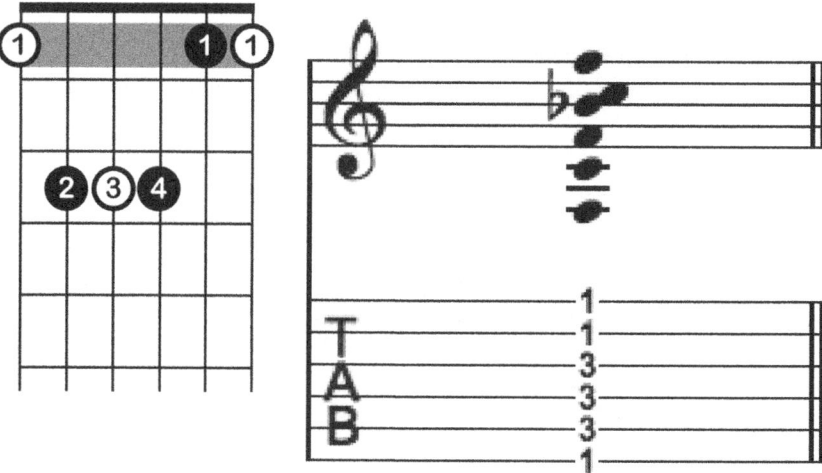

B♭sus4

The other movable sus4 shape has its root on the fifth string. Slide the little finger back one fret to create an ordinary B♭ barre shape, making the change from sus4 to major chord really easy.

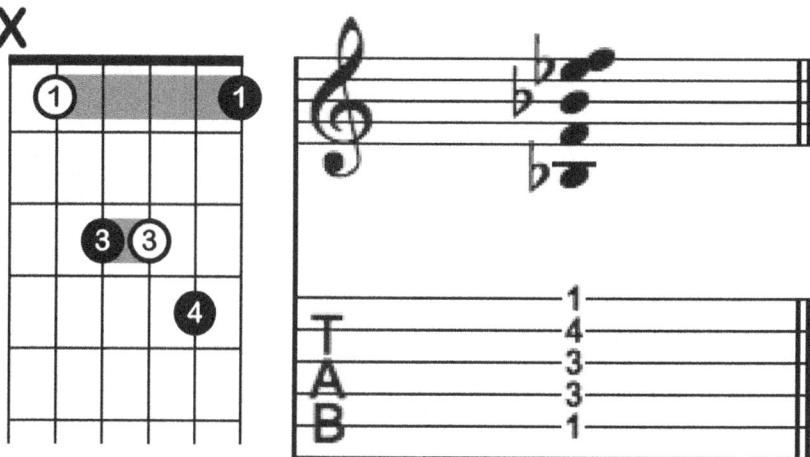

B♭sus2

This movable sus2 barre shape is a Frank Zappa favorite. Used in many of his compositions the sus2 became known as the secret Zappa chord. Resolve this shape to a major chord by simply adding the little finger.

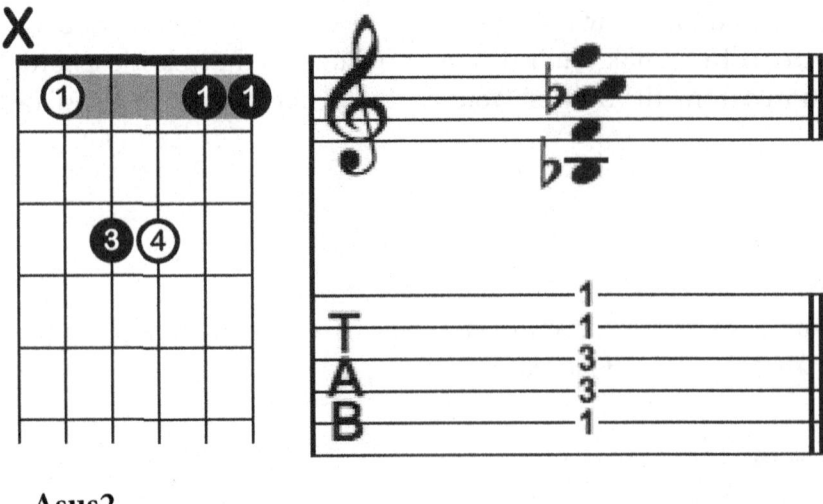

Asus2

Much beloved of acoustic-playing songwriters, Asus2 sounds more complicated and difficult than it really is. Try making up riffs using combinations of A, Asus4 (see below) and Asus2.

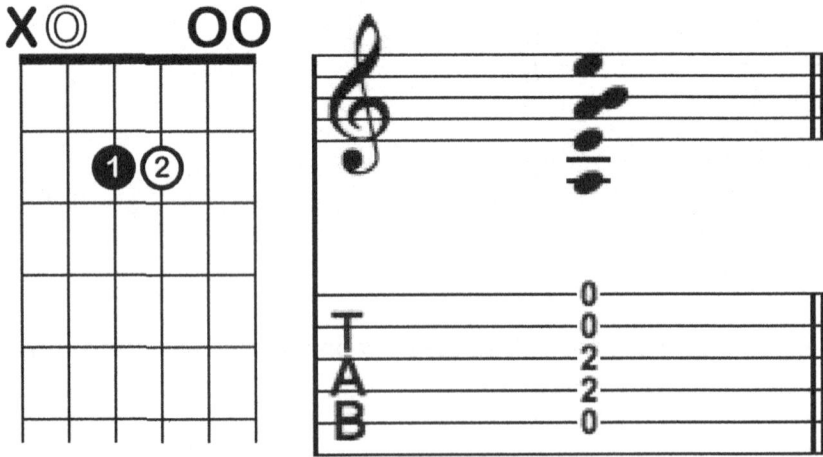

Asus4

If you're playing a song that starts on a chord of D, wait until you get to a chord of A in the music, and try playing Asus4, followed by A. This is called a resolution and is a useful songwriting tool.

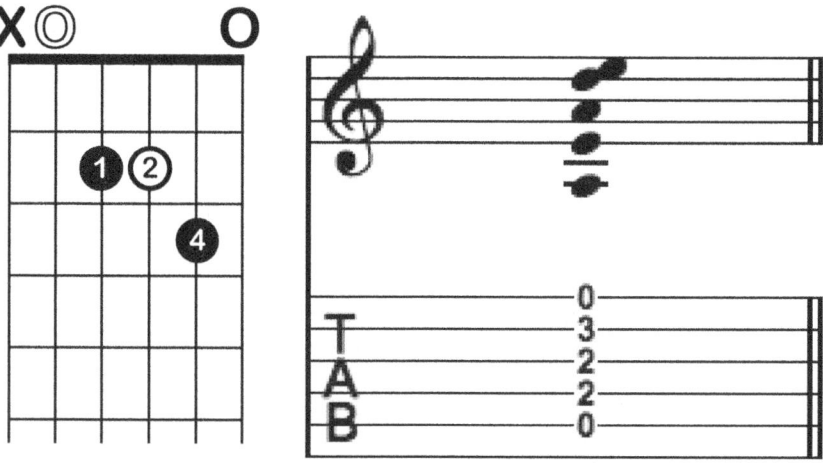

Bsus4

The note of B (at the 4th fret, third string) is doubled by the open second string, creating a 12-string guitar effect. This shape appears in Suzanne Vega's song "Luka."

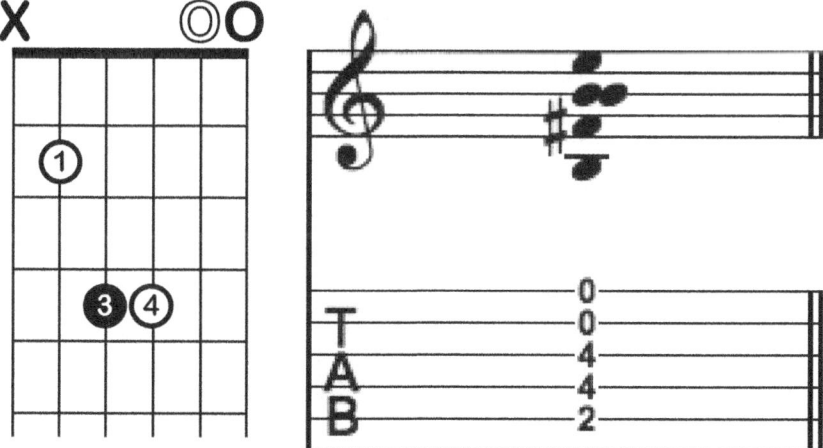

Csus4

As long as you only play the middle four strings, this is a much easier alternative than the barre shape Csus4 at the 3rd fret. If you use this fingering, it's easy to resolve to a normal C chord.

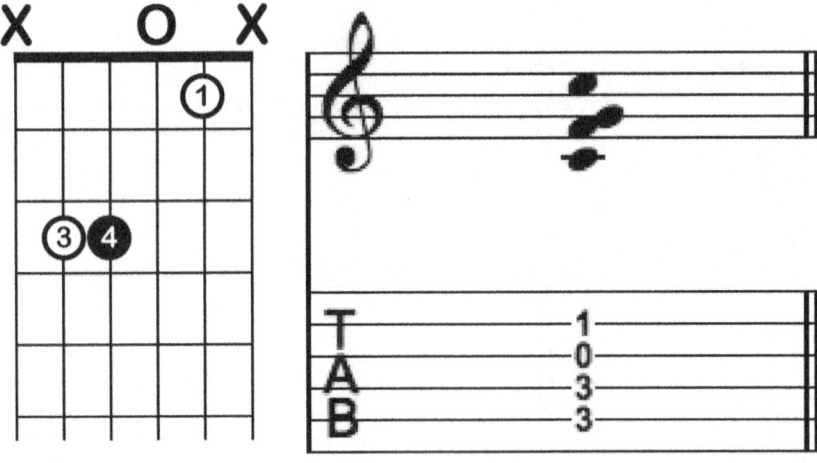

Dsus2

Play a D chord and take one finger off to create the chord of Dsus2. John Lennon used a combination of sus2, major, and sus4 chords like this to write "Happy Xmas (War Is Over)."

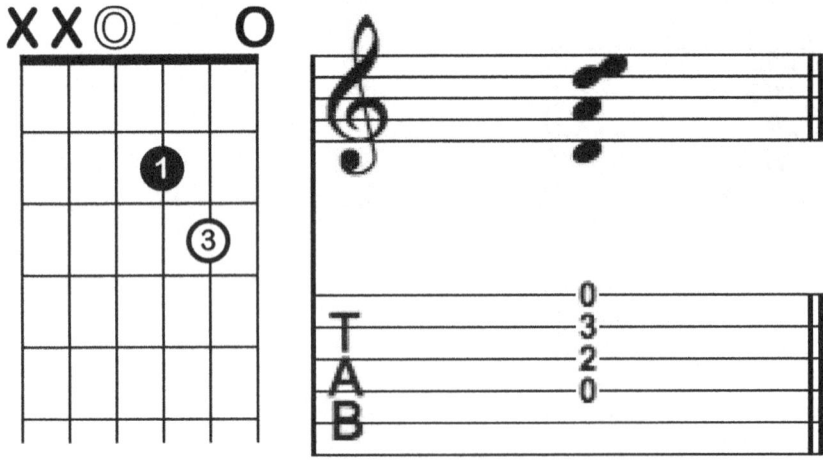

Dsus4

Many players like to keep their second finger at the 2ⁿᵈ fret on the first string (i.e. just one fret behind the little finger), in readiness for changing the Dsus4 back to a D.

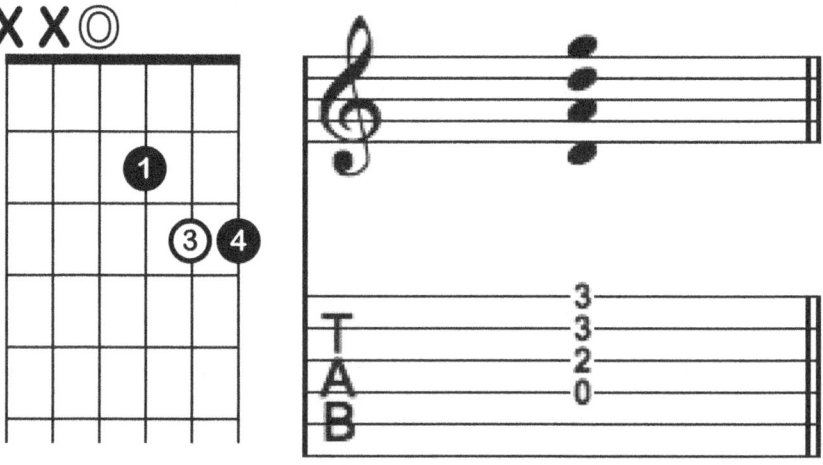

Esus4

A similar idea can apply to Esus4, which resolves easily to a straight chord of E. Bear in mind, though, that including the open third string actually creates a chord of Em, not Esus2.

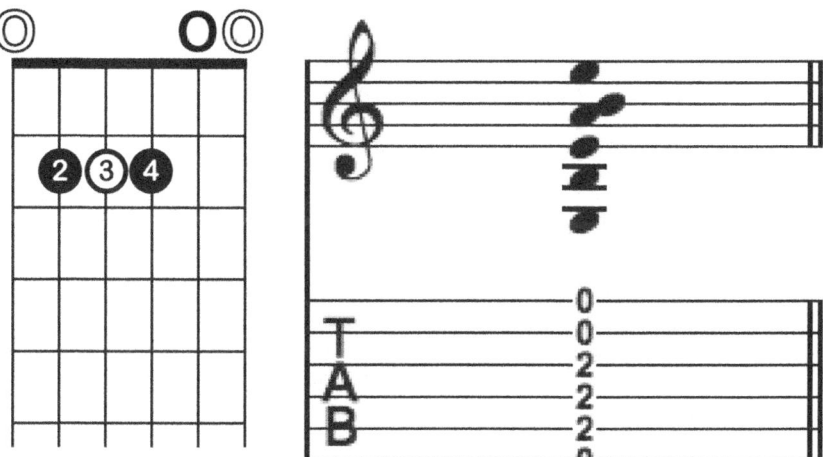

Gsus4

This less-used open sus4 chord is most useful if you're playing it on an acoustic, because it uses two open strings in the middle of the chord. Playing the first string is optional.

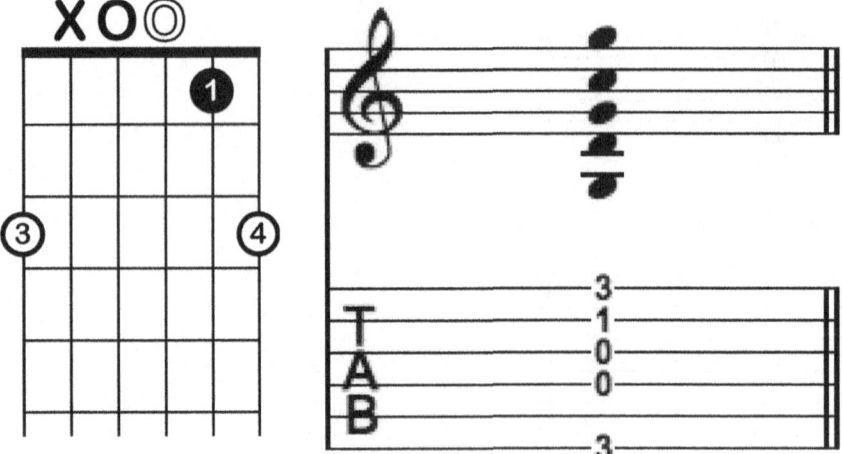

Other Useful Open Chords

Sometimes, a particular shape or fingering might create a chord with a complex-sounding name, even if it's really easy to play. Shown here are some of the common examples you may see in songbooks. These shapes are particularly good for acoustic songwriting because they sound colorful and complex, helping to suggest melodies and ideas. All of these examples contain at least one open string, and none of them use barres.

You may notice that most of these examples are simply familiar chords with one or more of the notes replaced by an open string. You can apply this idea to almost any chord you know—experiment and see what happens. *Quick Tip:* If it doesn't sound good, try moving the whole shape to a different fret position.

Aadd9

This chord is an addition of the open A chord shape, but take note of the finger number changes that are necessary to accommodate the stretch. This chord creates a laid-back, Joni Mitchell sound.

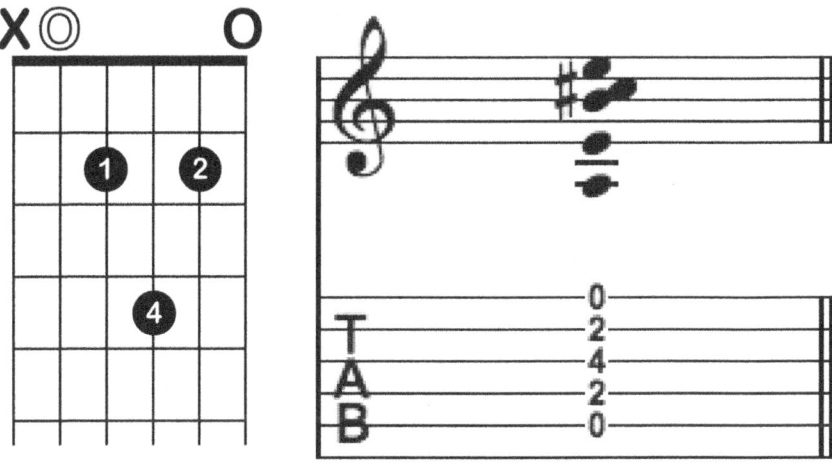

Cadd9

This is a C chord with the little finger added at the 3rd fret. It works especially well with songs which start or end on a G chord. The open first string can be omitted.

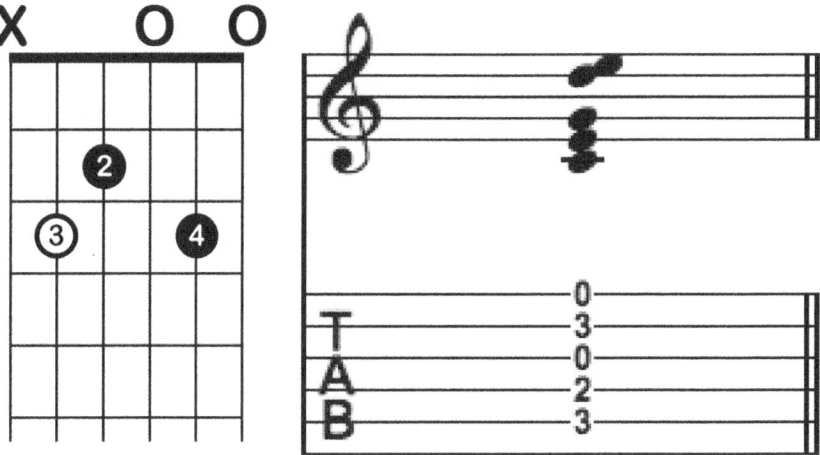

Em add9

Although this chord isn't that great if you just strum it up and down, try picking across the notes one at a time—that clash in the middle of the chord creates a heavy metal intro effect.

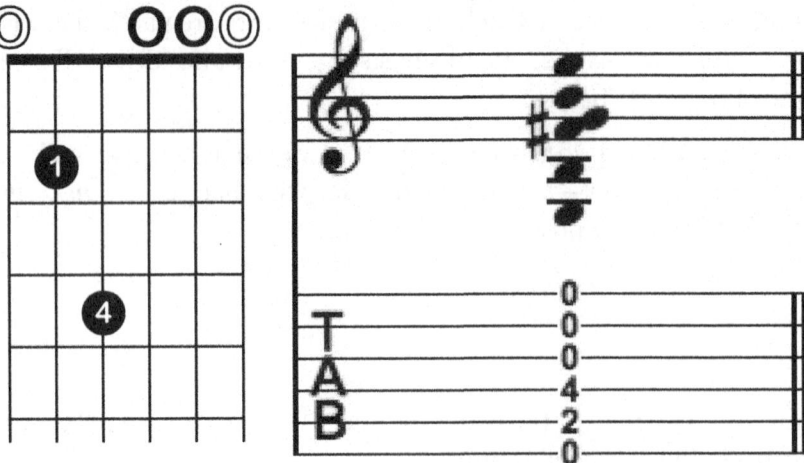

Fmaj7#11

Don't be put off by the jazzy-sounding name here—this is a great chord. Again, it's most effective when you pick the notes one at a time, but it also works with fingerstyle-picking techniques.

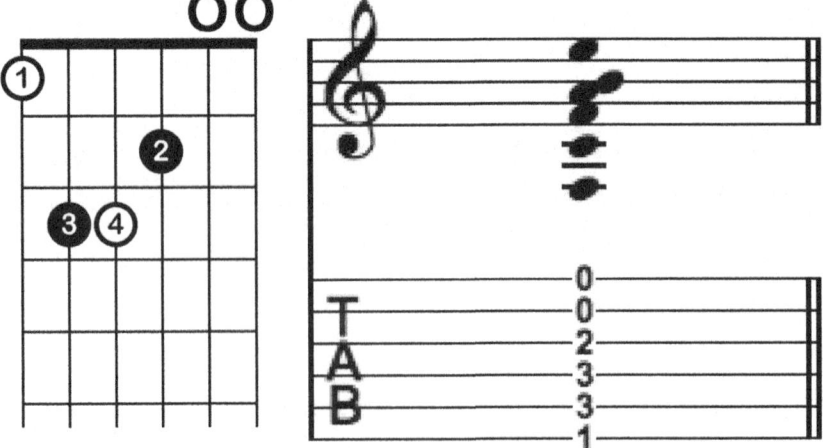

G6

If you move the Fmaj7 shown in the "Open Seventh Chords" section up two frets, you get this version of G6, as used by Keith Richards in the Rolling Stones' "Angie," and at the end of The Beatles' "She Loves You."

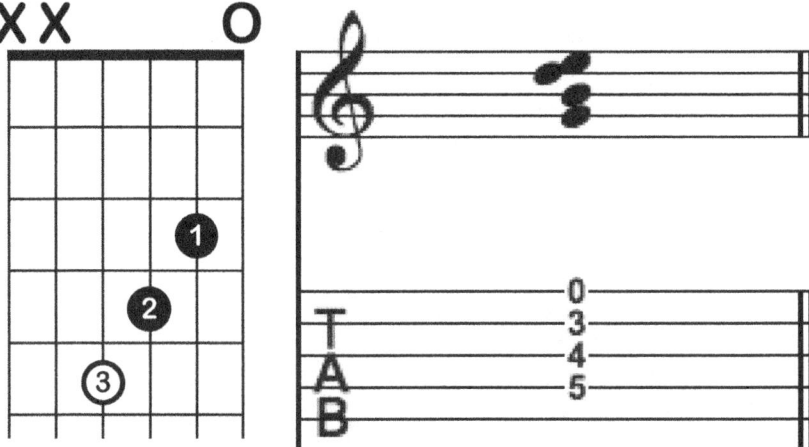

Slashed Chords

Many chord books and song transcriptions feature slashed chords, which confuses some guitarists because they don't know whether to play the chord on the left or the right of the slash. Here's how they work: The letter before the slash refers to the chord name itself; and the letter after is simply a single bass note. So A/G, for example, means a chord of A with a note of G in the bass. If you're playing in a band, it's normally OK for the guitarist to play the chord before the slash and the bass player to play the single bass note. If you're playing unaccompanied, you need to figure out a way to finger the chord and bass note—as shown some examples here. Remember, any chord can have an alternate bass note—try figuring out some of your own.

A/G

Although it's possible to play a straight A chord in the normal way and reach across with the little finger for the bass note, this version, with the first finger flattened across three strings, is much easier.

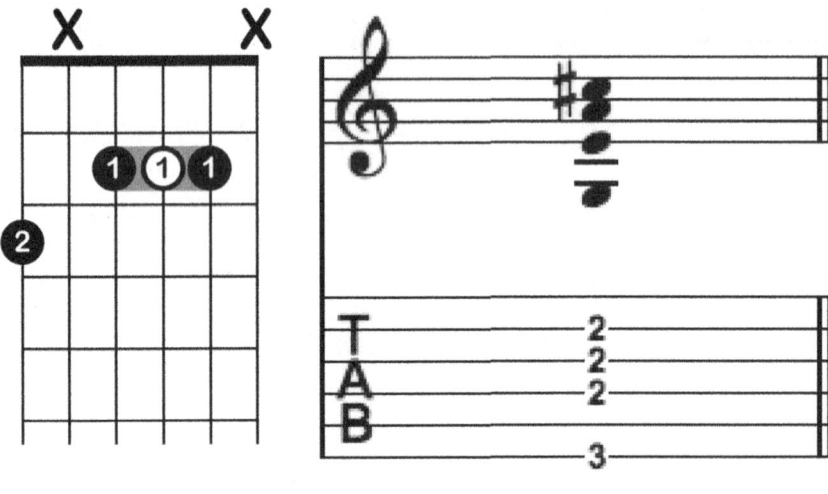

D/F♯

Some guitar teachers will give you a slap on the wrist for hanging your thumb over the top of the neck like this, but Jimi Hendrix, Paul Simon, and dozens of folk and blues players use this technique.

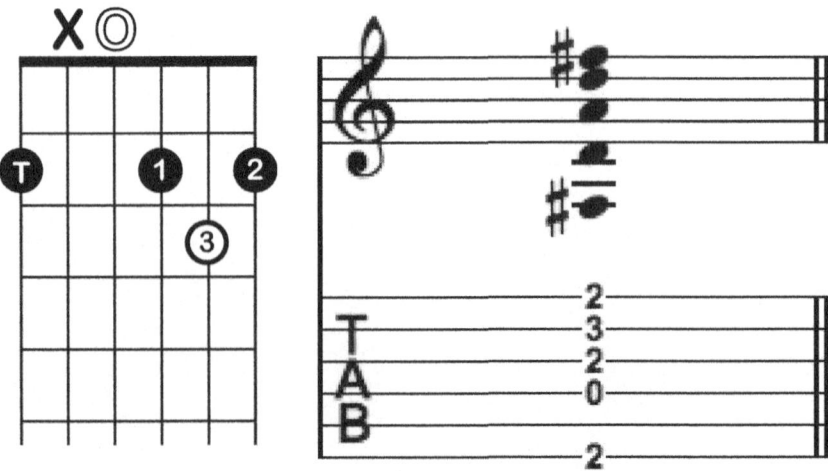

G/A

This chord uses an open string for the bass note. The chord of G/A is sometimes referred to as A11, and it has a very warm, jazzy sound.

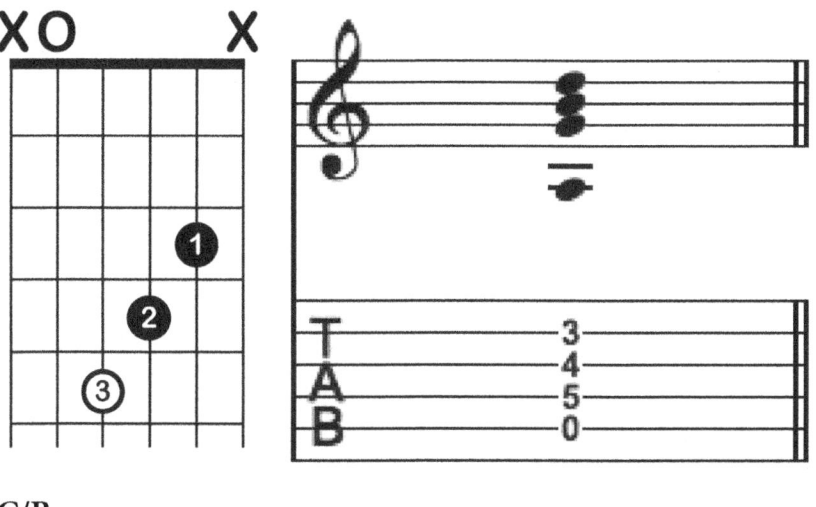

C/B

Here, the root note of an ordinary C chord has simply been dropped down a fret. Paul Simon uses it in the acoustic rhythm part from Simon & Garfunkel's hit "America."

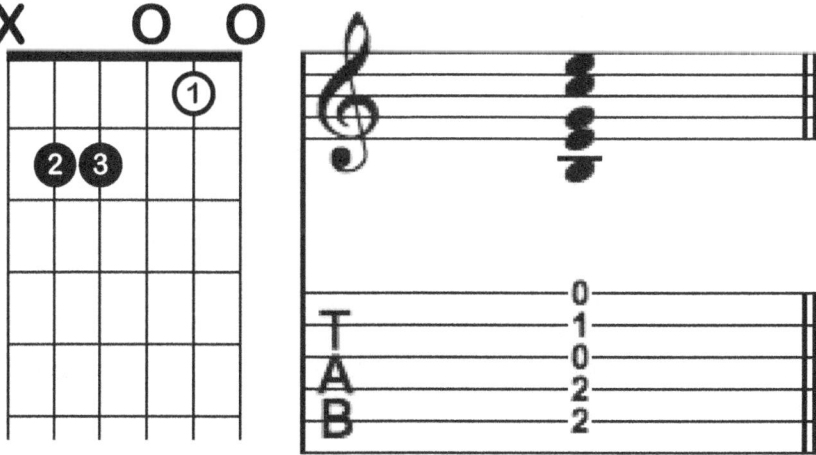

D/C

As with the A/G (above), the side of the little finger is used to stop an open string from sounding. It's the second chord in the verse of The Beatles' "Dear Prudence."

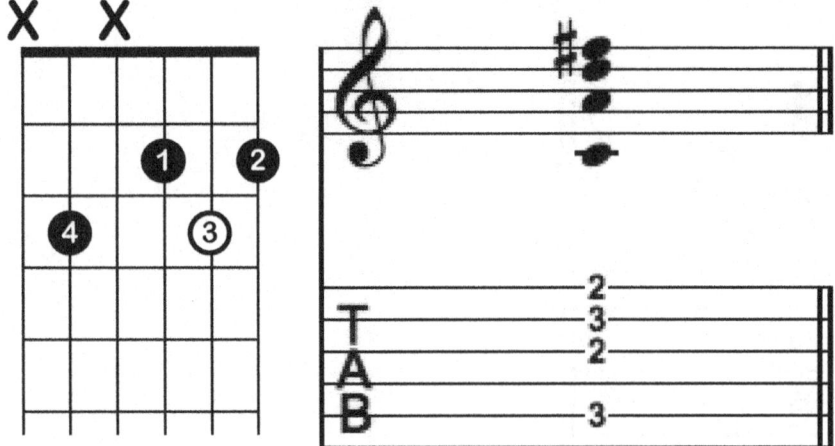

Alternative Chord Shapes

Playing a rhythm part doesn't always mean using the shapes you'll find in a chord encyclopedia. Lots of pro players use less conventional shapes, either because they work better in the context of a band mix; because they're more convenient to play at the time; or simply because they prefer the sound. This section includes two movable chords which chord books sometimes miss out, plus examples of partial chords. Basically, a partial chord simply means missing out on some of the notes of the chord—usually the lower ones in the bass range. Players as diverse as Nile Rogers of Chic, Prince, and Eric Clapton have all used partial chords at one time or another. Any chord can be played as a partial shape.

D7 a/k/a "Middle D7"

So-called because it doesn't use the outer two strings, this fretted shape is handy in many different styles, though it's perhaps most common in Rock and Roll or Rhythm and Blues.

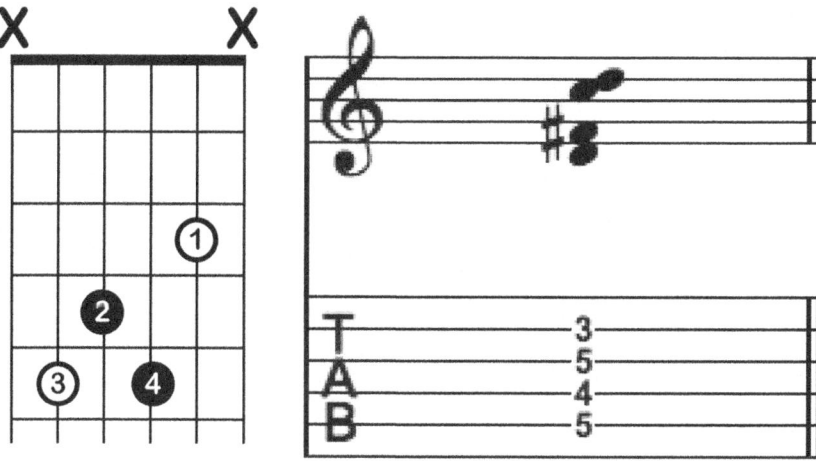

D "The Folky C Shape"

If you look carefully you'll notice that this is just a C chord moved up two frets, with a barre over the first three strings. Many players actually prefer this version to a conventional barre chord shape.

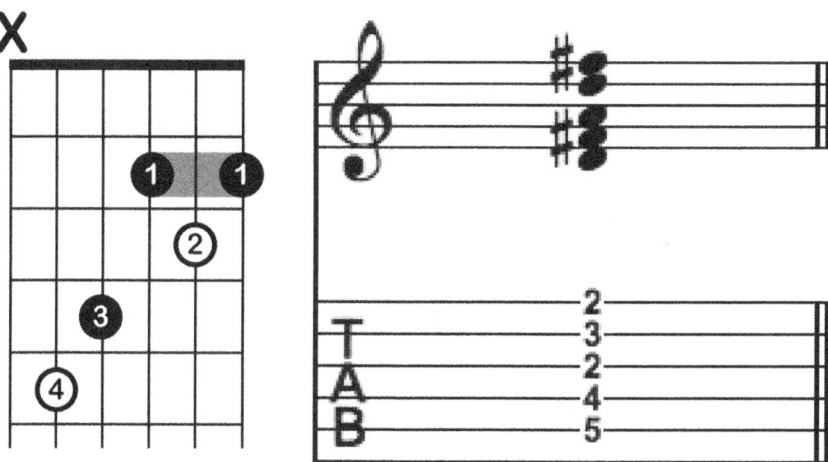

F (partial)

The simplest way to create a partial chord is to look at any chord you already know—and don't play all of the notes. This is a chord of F with some of the lower notes removed.

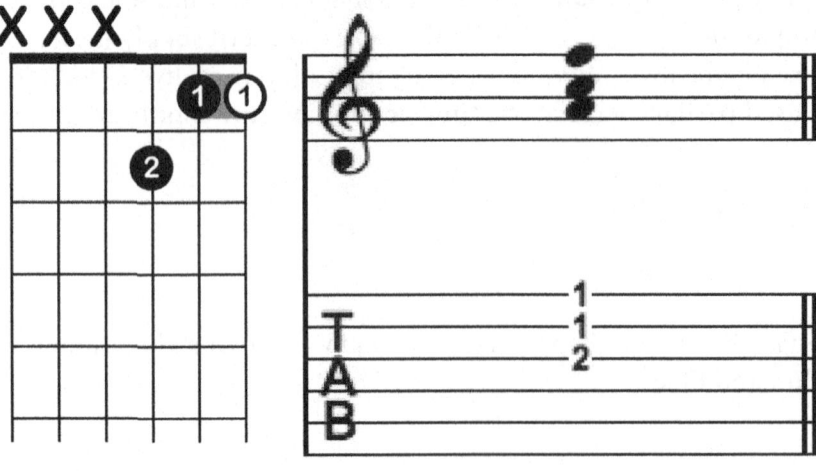

Dm (partial)

This chord is based on a Dm barre at the 5th fret, but because you're not playing any of the bass notes, you don't need the barre. Try playing this shape while someone else plays an ordinary Dm.

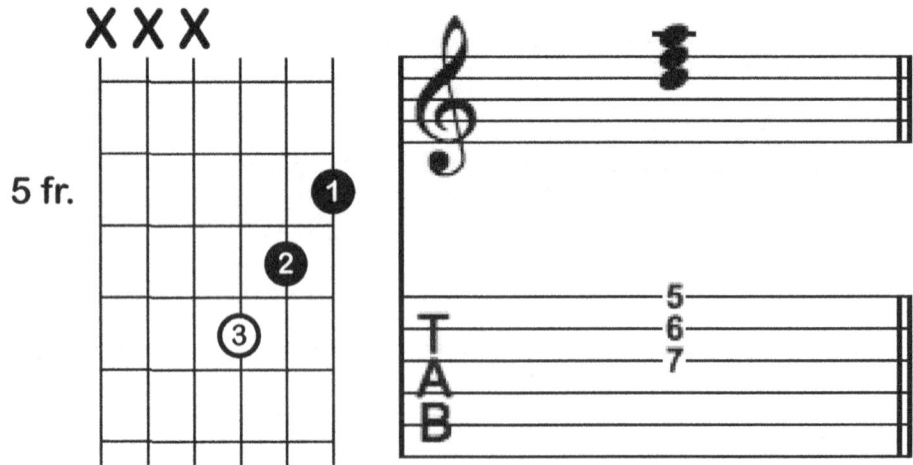

A7 (partial)

Although this isn't based on a conventional barre chord, it's still a valid seventh chord shape—it's basically an open D7 chord (as shown in the "Open Seventh Chords" section) moved up 7 frets.

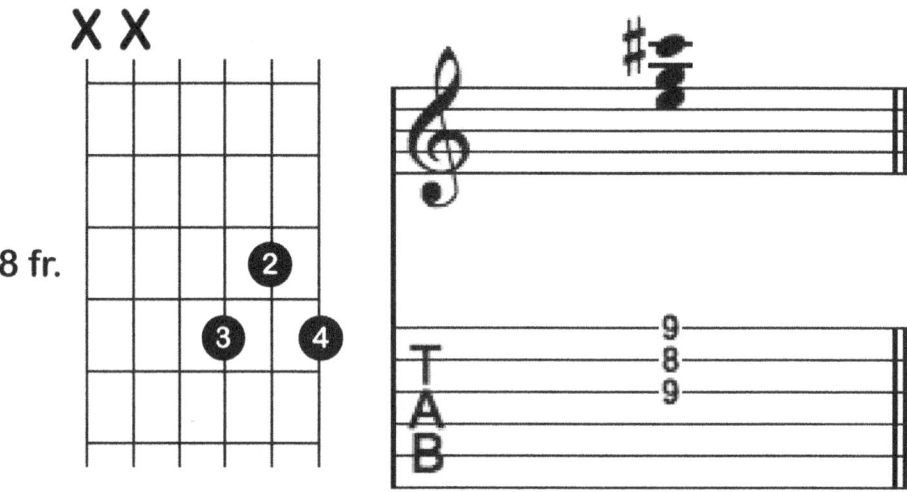

Classic Chords

There are a small number of chords that have become classics in their own right because they're instantly recognizable. The examples shown here have all been associated with a particular song, and some have been the subject of much debate among guitarists as to how they should be played. Each of them should be identifiable if you just strum across the whole chord once.

Don't be put off by the fact that many of these chords have complex-sounding, theoretical names—people are far more likely to know a chord as "the ending of James Bond" than they are to care about it being called E minor with a major 9. The nature of these chords is such that their character really comes to life when played on the guitar yet loses something when played on other instruments such as piano.

G7sus4/A "A Hard Day's Night"

This may sound slightly different from the Beatles' record because it was originally played on an electric 12-string. Nevertheless, this is how George Harrison played it, back in 1964.

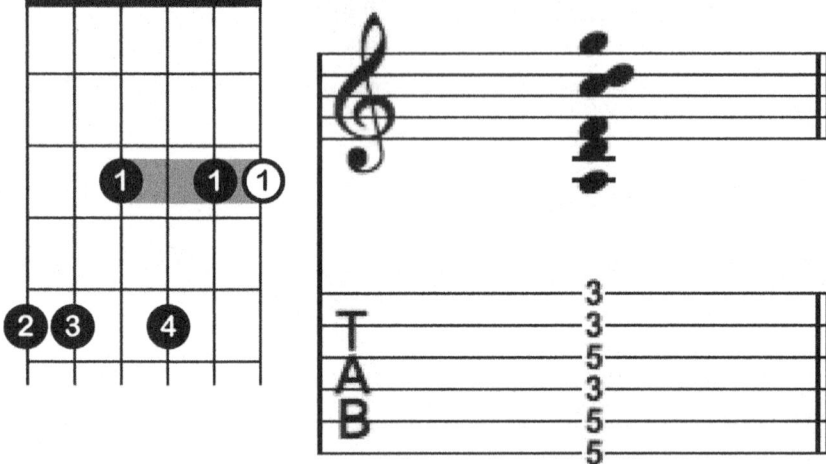

Dm7add11 "Walkin' on the Moon"

This Police song would not have been complete without the "chang" of this great-sounding chord on Andy Summers' Fender Telecaster. Add a C barre chord and you can play along with the bass riff.

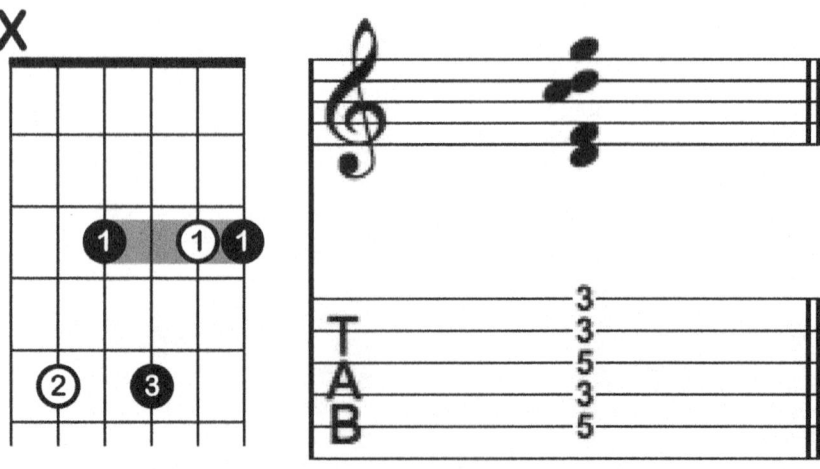

Em(maj9) " The 007 Chord"

The James Bond Theme ends with this ominous-sounding chord, played in 1960 by session guitarist Vic Flick. Use the side of the fretting hand's first finger to mute the first string.

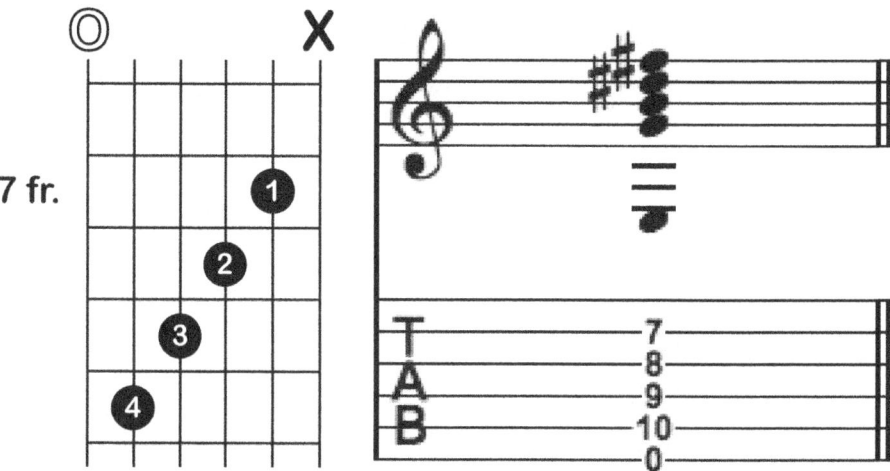

E7♯9 "The Hendrix chord'"

"Foxy Lady," "Purple Haze," "Voodoo Chile (Slight Return)"… All three of these Jimi Hendrix classics have featured this chord. The open first and sixth strings are optional in each case, making the chord sound fuller.

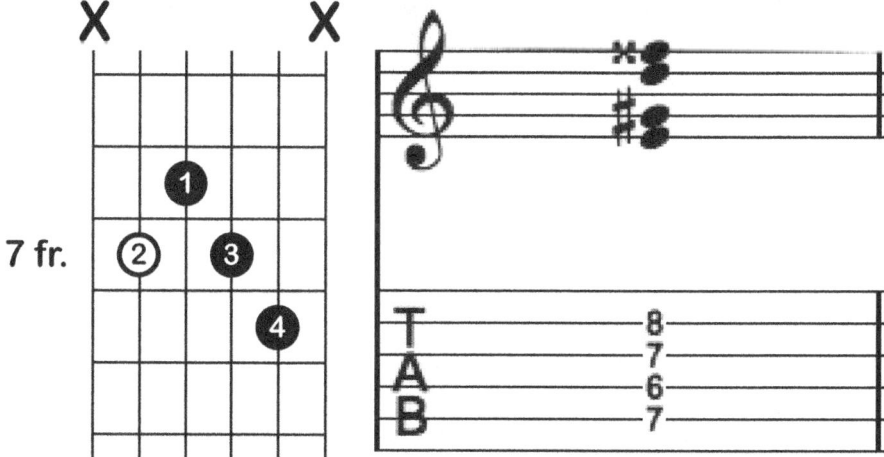

D+ "No Particular Place to Go"

This partial augmented chord, played up and down rapidly a total of 13 times, forms the intro to Chuck Berry's famous rock 'n' roll tune. The rest of the song uses chords of G7, C7 and D7.

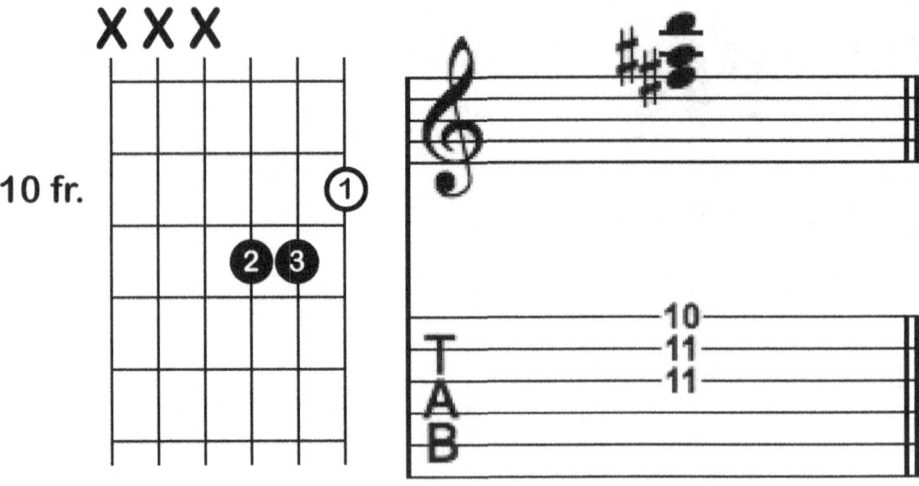

Cmaj7 "Design for Life"

Pick across the strings one by one, starting on the root note, until you get used to the second string, then pick back in the other direction. It's the first part of the Manic Street Preachers' "Design for Life."

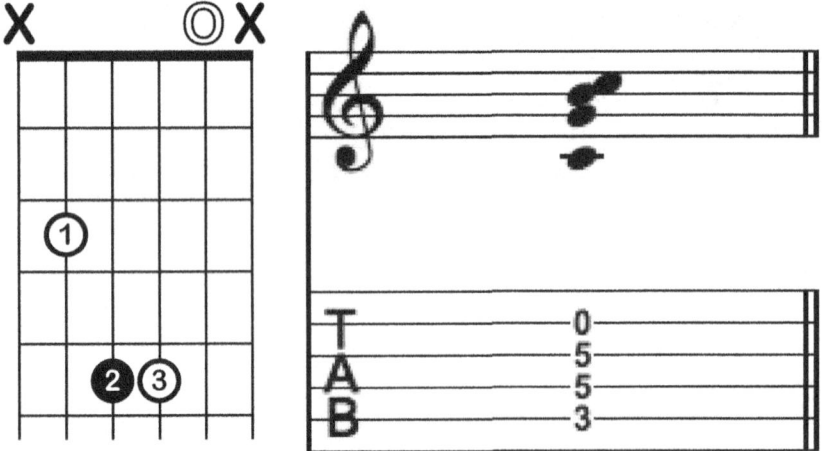

D & Dsus4

Play a normal D chord, then add and remove the little finger at the third fret (shown in grey) while you're strumming. That's the intro to this Queen single, from their 1980 album *The Game*.

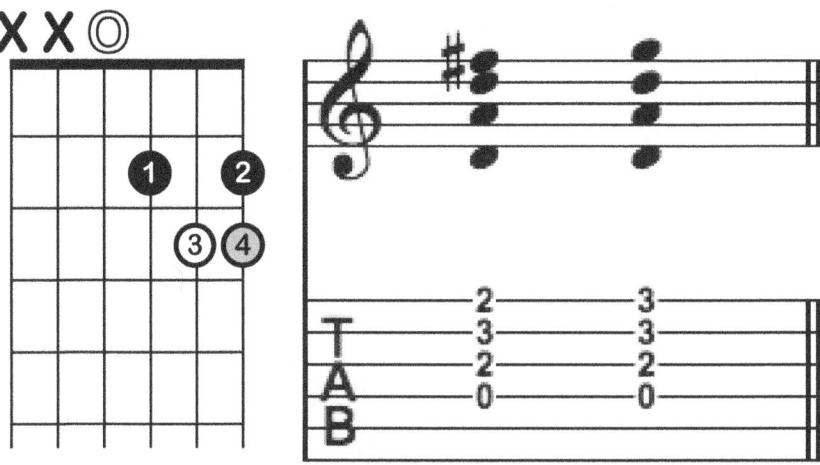

E/D "Hole Hearted"

Play a D chord twice, then slide it up two frets and pick the strings one by one. Nuno Bettencourt plays this on an acoustic just before the verse section from Extreme's hit, "Hole Hearted."

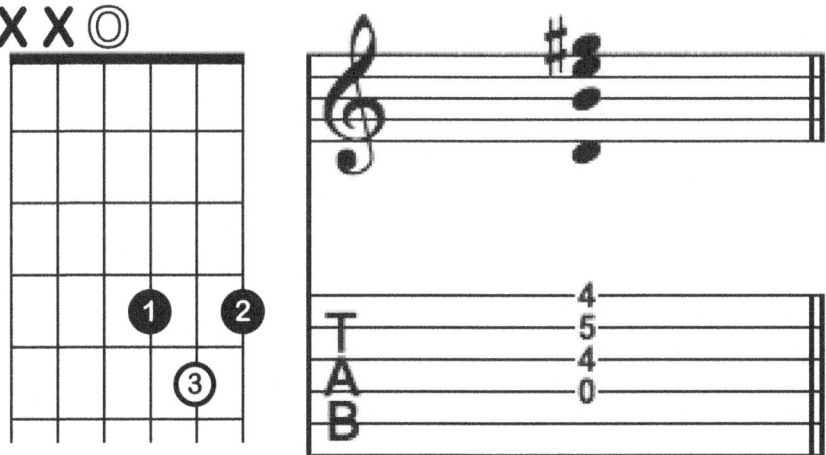

E5 "Paranoid"

Because of the partial barre behind two of the fretted notes, you can play hammer-ons between the 7th and 9th fret, as Tony Iommi does in the intro from this early Black Sabbath recording.

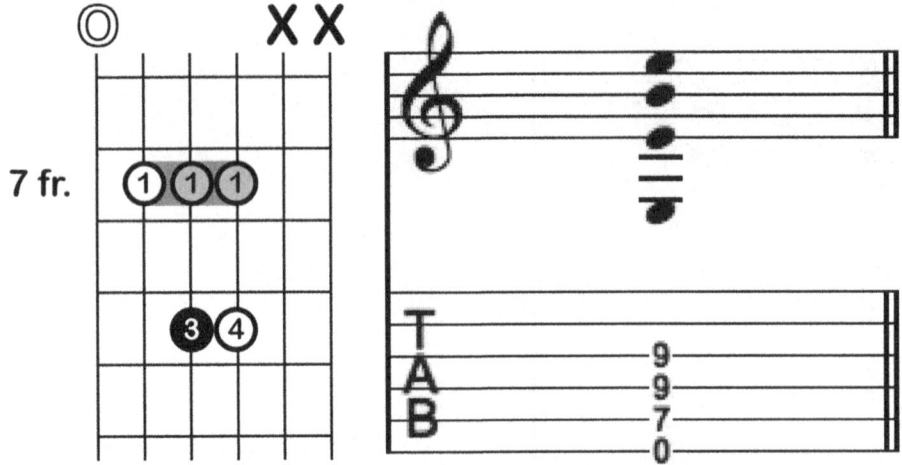

E9 "The James Brown Chord"

This funky ninth chord shape appears in a long list of James Brown tunes, and is one of the most commonly-used chords in '70s funk and disco. Try sliding up to the chord as you strum rapidly.

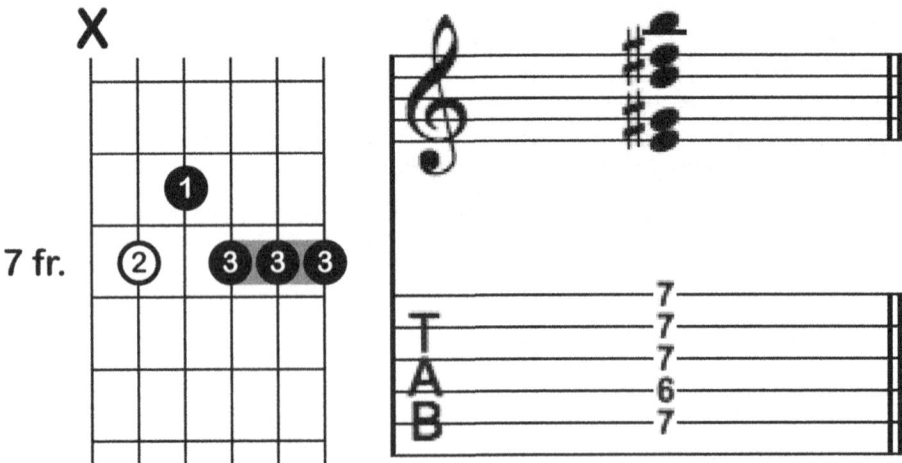

Bsus4 & B "Pinball Wizard"

You need to reach the thumb over the top of the neck to reach the bass note here. Use fast up and down strums while you add and remove the little finger note at the 9th fret.

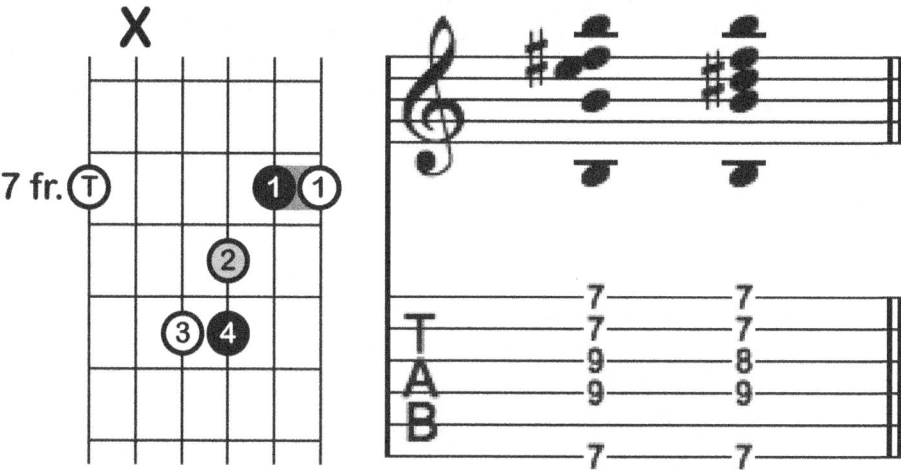

C♯5add9 "Message in a Bottle"

Here's another chord from a Police track. Most of the time, when 5add9 type chords appear in a song, they're picked one note at a time rather than strummed right across.

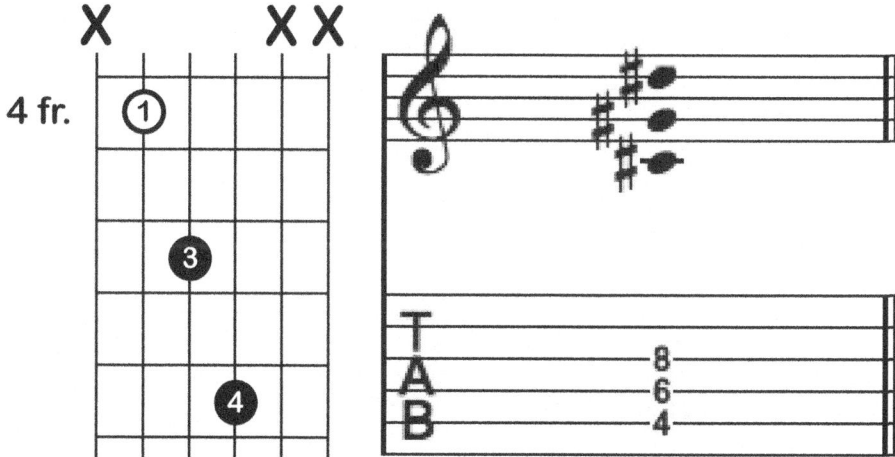

A & D/A "All Right Now"

The D/A shape is played after a straight A chord in one of Paul Kossoff's guitar parts from this track by '70s rock-blues band Free. It also appears in Queen's "Hammer to Fall" and many AC/DC classics.

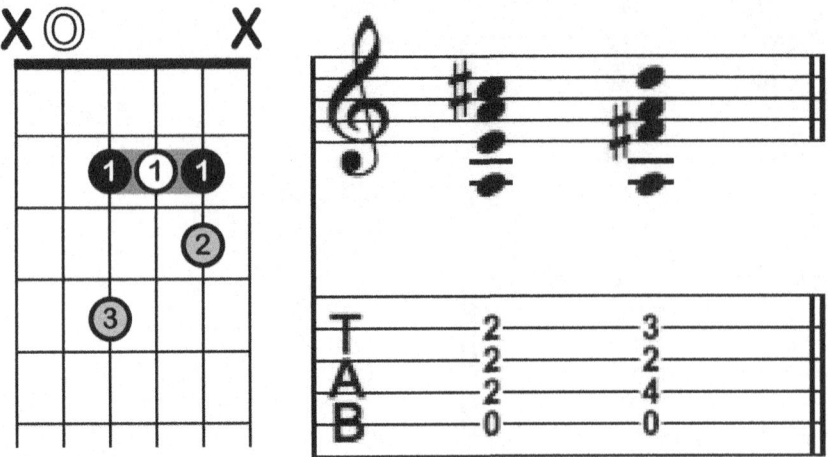

Fsus2 "Live Forever"

At the end of the chorus from this early Oasis hit, Noel Gallagher cranks up the distortion levels as he picks out a riff using the notes from this open-chord shape. It also appears in the chorus of Peter Frampton's "Do You Feel Like I Do."

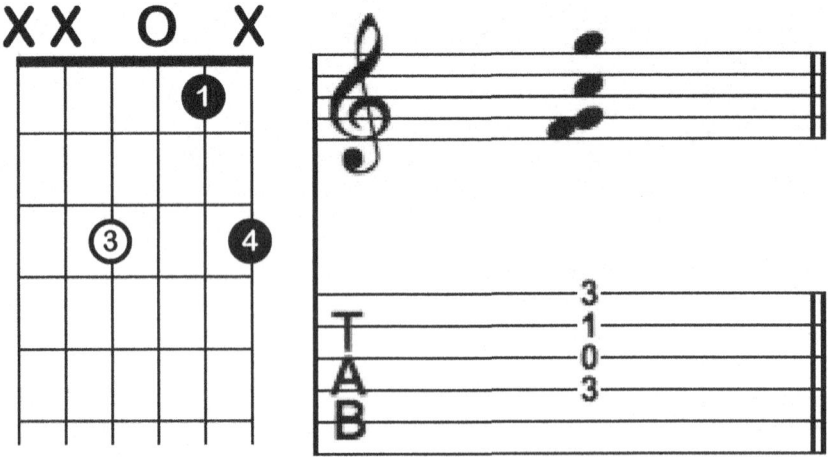

Playing Chords

Many aspiring candidates find rhythm playing their weakest area. When you consider that your average working guitarist spends around 95% of the time playing chord accompaniment, it seems odd that some players only ever want to learn riffs or solos. There are many styles of music—rock 'n' roll, R&B, reggae, indie-rock, Brit-pop; even some rock and jazz—where the guitarist hardly ever plays a solo.

Listed below are some bits of advice to help you maintain and improve the standard of your chord playing. There is also an explanation of some of the common naming conventions that musicians may use when writing out chord charts for guitar players.

Rhythm Tips

Here are a couple of things to keep in mind when practicing your rhythm playing or working on accompaniment parts:

- **Keep it simple.** Sometimes just two or three notes will sound better than a full chord.

- **One at a time.** Arpeggio techniques—i.e. picking out the notes of a chord one by one in time with the music—can make a rhythm guitar part more interesting.

- **Don't' fight the power.** In rock music, especially if you're using distortion, power chords usually work better than other types.

- **Right under your fingers.** When you're using barre chords, don't just move an F shape up and down the neck. You may find there's a B♭ shape which is easier to get to.

- **X doesn't mark the spot.** If a string is marked with an X in the fretbox, it's very important that you don't play it, because it will interfere with the sound of the chord.

- **Don't squeeze.** If you get fret buzz in a chord, move the fingers closer to the next fret—that way you'll need less pressure to get the strings sounding clearly.

- **Always keep going.** When learning a piece of music from a chart, don't stop and pause every time there's a difficult chord change. Attempt the whole piece at a slower tempo so you keep the changes in time. The speed will come with practice.

- **Get out there.** Play with other musicians and singers whenever you can—it's the best and quickest way to improve your timing, technique and chord knowledge.

Naming Conventions

Because of the different styles of guitarists throughout the world, several notation "standards" have evolved. Below are several examples, all shown with a root note of C. On the left is printed the way you'll see chords in this chart (usually the most common), followed by alternate namings.

C	C major, Cmaj
Cm	Cmin, C-
C7	Cdom7
Cmaj7	CM7, Ctriangle, Ctriangle7
Cm7	Cmin7, C-7

C5   C(no 3rd)

C+   Caug, C5+

C7♯9   C7(-10), C7(sharp10)

Finally, if you don't know a chord, there's usually one that you do know which will fit just as well. Here are a few tips;

- Chords ending with 9, 11 or 13 can usually be replaced with an equivalent 7th; *e.g.*, if you don't know Cm11, Cm7 will work fine. If you can't play C9, try C7, and so on.

- In most cases, straight major or minor chords will work instead of 7s or 9s.

- Power chords (*e.g.* C5, A5 *etc.*) can be used as a substitute for any major or minor chord, including 7s, 9s, *etc.*

Updates!

Please sign up for notifications. We frequently have subscriber specials and updates to products. You will not get spam, we hate it as well!

https://hjjpublishing.com/

Made in the USA
Middletown, DE
29 November 2019